For Engineers & Designers

NANOCAD Exercises

200 3D PRACTICE DRAWINGS

SACHIDANAND JHA

Dear Reader,

Thank you for choosing **NANOCAD Exercises** book. This book is part of a family of premium-quality CADIN360 books, all of which are written by Outstanding author who combine practical experience with a gift for teaching.

CADIN360 was founded in 2016. More than 3 years later, we're still committed to producing consistently exceptional books. With each of our titles, we're working hard to set a new standard for the industry. From the paper we print on, to the authors we work with, our goal is to bring you the best books available.

I hope you see all that reflected in these pages. I'd be very interested to hear your comments and get your feedback on how we're doing. Feel free to let me know what you think about this or any other CADIN360 book by sending me an email at contactus@cadin360.com.

If you think you've found a technical error in this book, please visit
https://cadin360.com/contact-us/.
Customer feedback is critical to our efforts at CADIN360.

Best regards,

Sachidanand Jha
Founder & CEO, CADIN360

NANOCAD Exercises

Published by
CADIN360
cadin360.com
Copyright © 2019 by CADIN360, All rights reserved.

Preface

NANOCAD Exercises

❖ This book contain 200 CAD practice exercises and drawings.

❖ This book does not provide step by step tutorial to design 3D models.

❖ S.I Unit is used.

❖ Predominantly used Third Angle Projection.

❖ This book is for **NANOCAD** and Other Feature-Based Modeling Software such as Inventor, SolidWorks, NX, Solid Edge, AutoCAD, PTC Creo etc.

❖ It is intended to provide Drafters, Designers and Engineers with enough 3D CAD exercises for practice on **NANOCAD**.

❖ It includes almost all types of exercises that are necessary to provide, clear, concise and systematic information required on industrial machine part drawings.

❖ Third Angle Projection is intentionally used to familiarize Drafters, Designers and Engineers in Third Angle Projection to meet the expectation of world wide Engineering drawing print.

❖ Clear and well drafted drawing help easy understanding of the design.

❖ This book is for Beginner, Intermediate and Advance CAD users.

❖ These exercises are from Basics to Advance level.

❖ Each exercises can be assigned and designed separately.

❖ No Exercise is a prerequisite for another. All dimensions are in mm.

❖ Note: Assume any missing dimensions.

EX-01

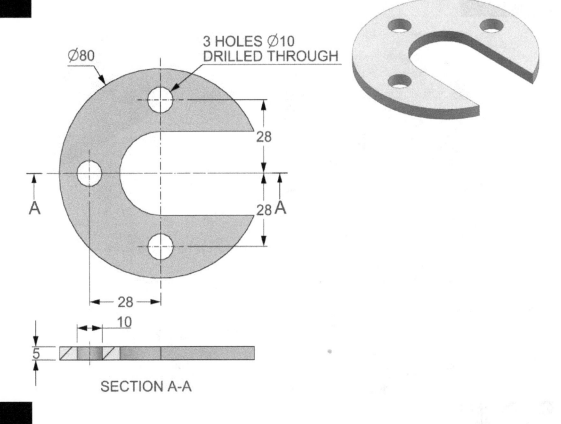

Ø80

3 HOLES Ø10
DRILLED THROUGH

28

28 A

A

28

10

5

SECTION A-A

EX-02

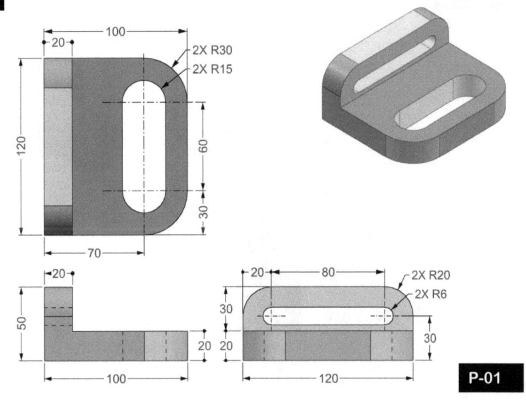

100

20

2X R30

2X R15

120

60

30

70

20

50

20

100

20 80

2X R20

2X R6

30

30

20 20

120

P-01

EX-03

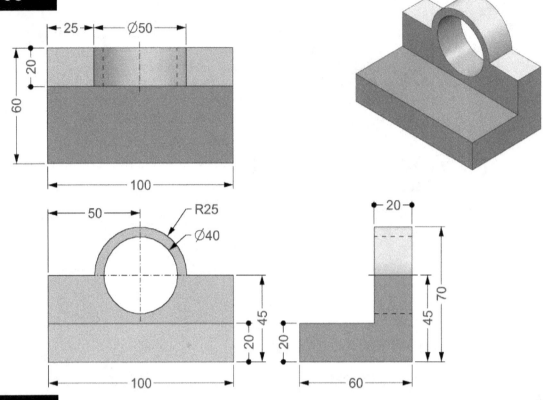

EX-04

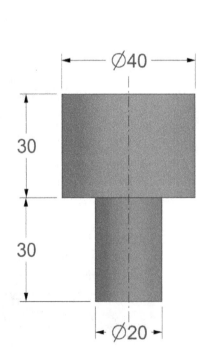

P-02

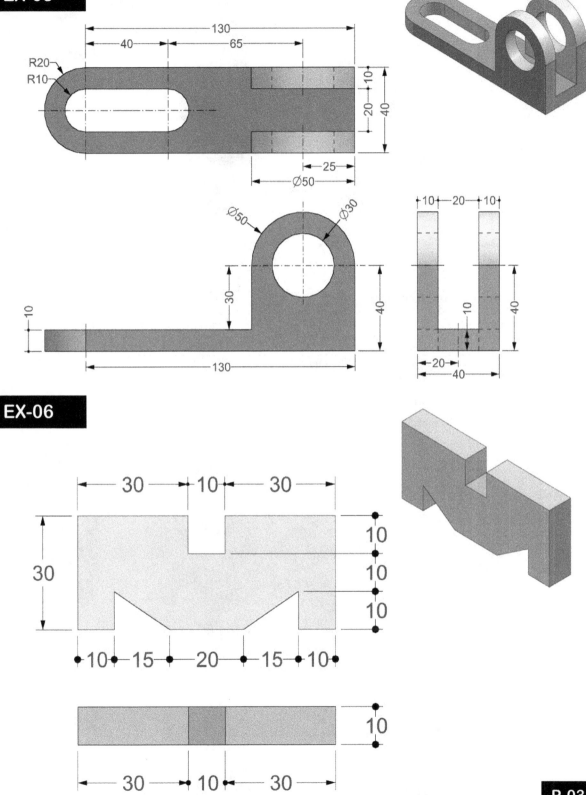

EX-05

EX-06

P-03

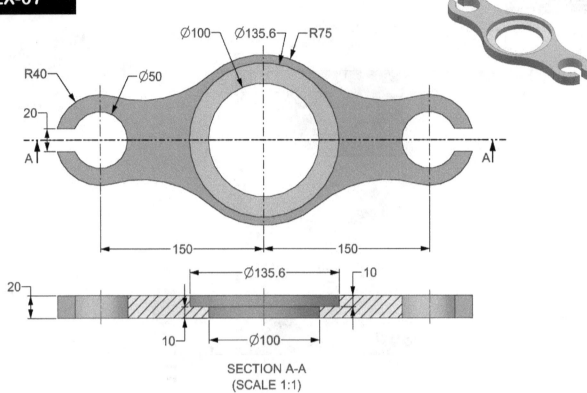

SECTION A-A
(SCALE 1:1)

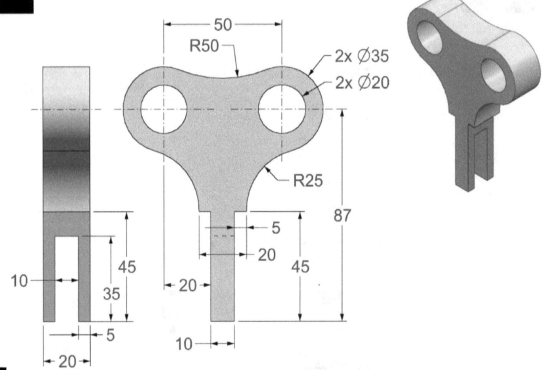

EX-09

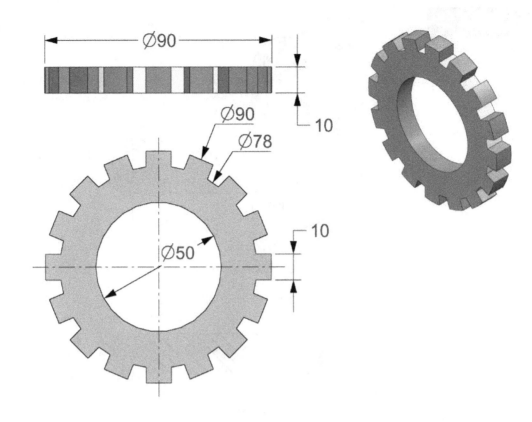

Ø90

10

Ø90
Ø78

10

Ø50

EX-10

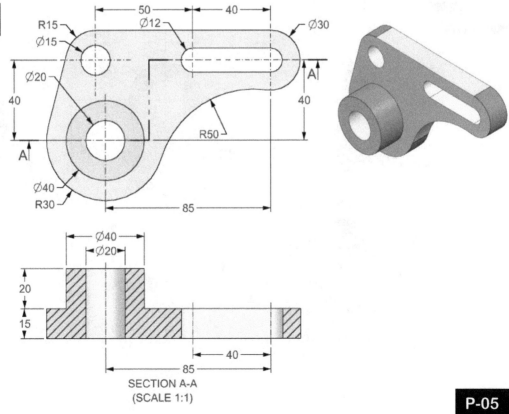

50   40

R15
Ø15
Ø12
Ø30

Ø20

A

40

40

R50

A

Ø40
R30

85

Ø40
Ø20

20

15

40

85

SECTION A-A
(SCALE 1:1)

EX-11

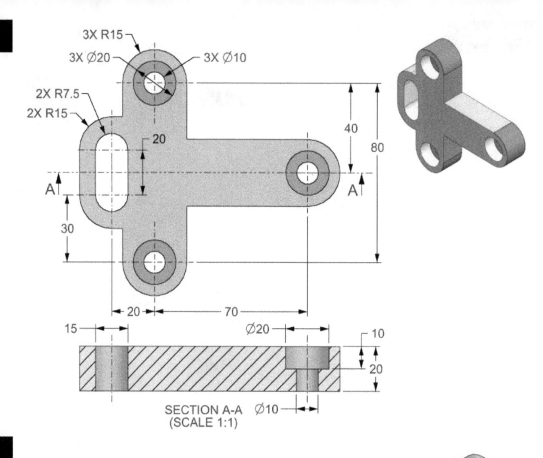

3X R15
3X Ø20
3X Ø10
2X R7.5
2X R15
20
40
80
A
30
20
70
15
Ø20
10
20
SECTION A-A
(SCALE 1:1)
Ø10
A

EX-12

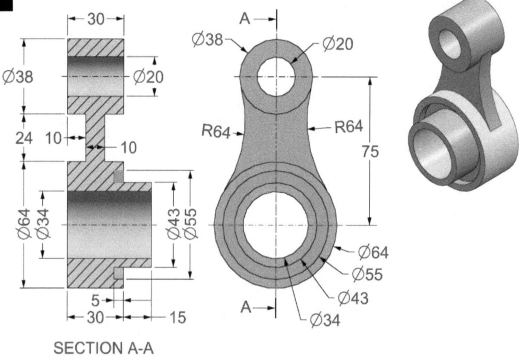

30
Ø38
Ø20
24   10
10
Ø64
Ø34
Ø43
Ø55
5
30
15

A
Ø38
Ø20
R64
R64
75
Ø64
Ø55
Ø43
A
Ø34

SECTION A-A
(SCALE 1:1)

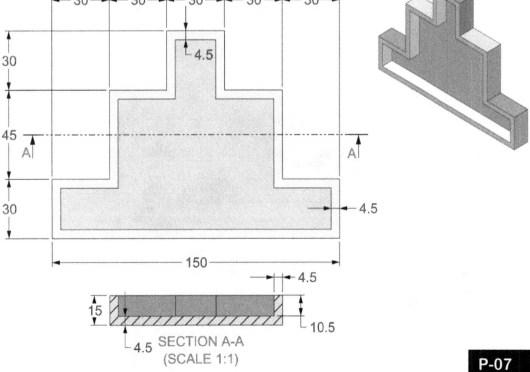

10   50

10   30

2X R5

2X ∅10

R10   15

40   40   30   20

5

40   20

20   30

70

30   30   30   30   30

30

4.5

45

A   A

30

4.5

150

4.5

15   10.5

4.5   SECTION A-A
(SCALE 1:1)

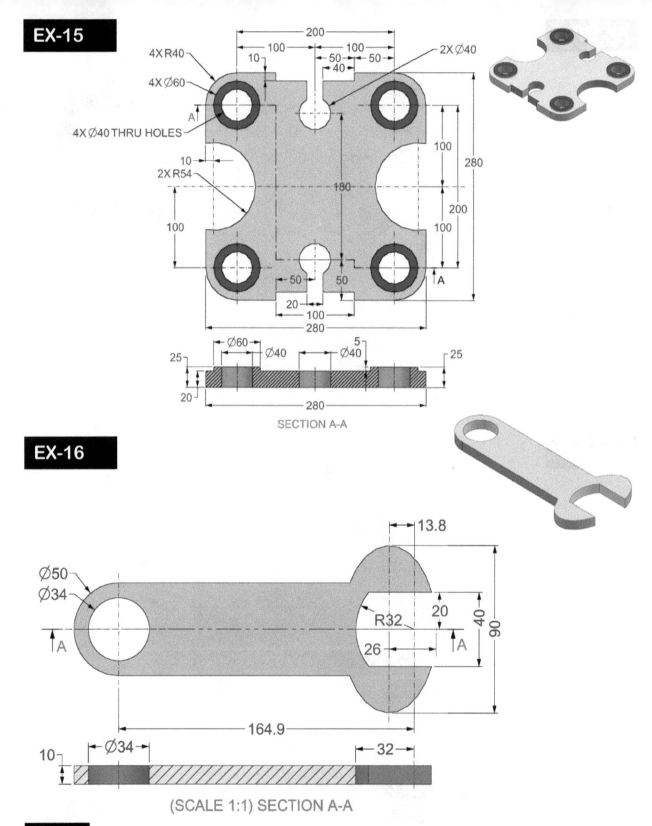

EX-15

4X R40
4X Ø60
4X Ø40 THRU HOLES
2X Ø40
2X R54

200
100
100
10
50
50
40
100
280
180
200
100
100
10
100
50
50
20
100
280

SECTION A-A

Ø60
Ø40
Ø40
5
25
25
20
280

EX-16

Ø50
Ø34
13.8
20
40
R32
26
90
A
A
164.9

Ø34
32
10

(SCALE 1:1) SECTION A-A

P-08

EX-17

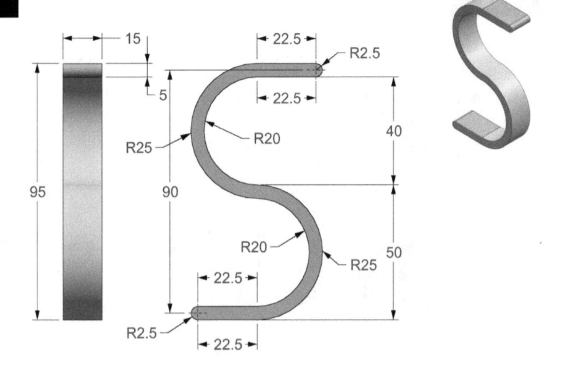

15

22.5
R2.5
22.5
5
R25 R20
40
95
90
R20
50
R25
22.5
R2.5
22.5

EX-18

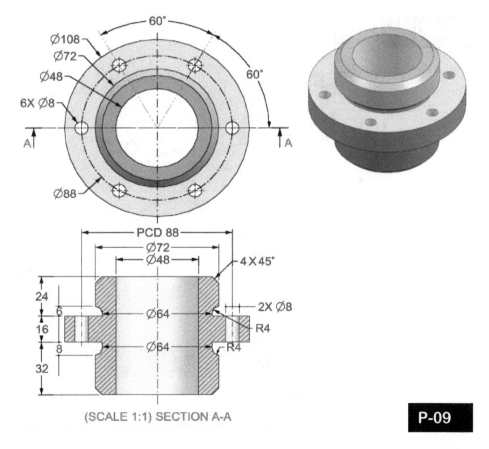

60°
Ø108
Ø72
Ø48
6X Ø8
60°
A
A
Ø88

PCD 88
Ø72
Ø48
4 X 45°
24
6
Ø64
2X Ø8
16
R4
8
Ø64
R4
32

(SCALE 1:1) SECTION A-A

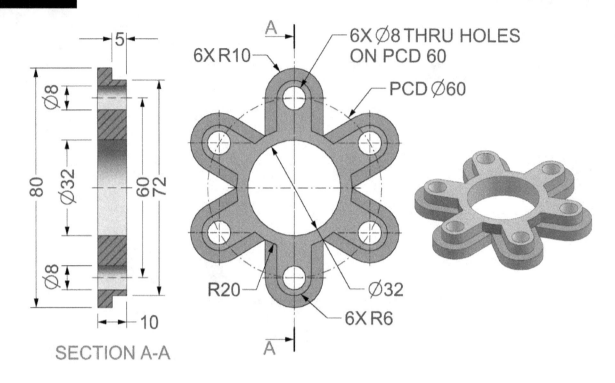

6X R10

6X Ø8 THRU HOLES ON PCD 60

PCD Ø60

5

Ø8

Ø32

80

60

72

Ø8

10

R20

Ø32

6X R6

SECTION A-A

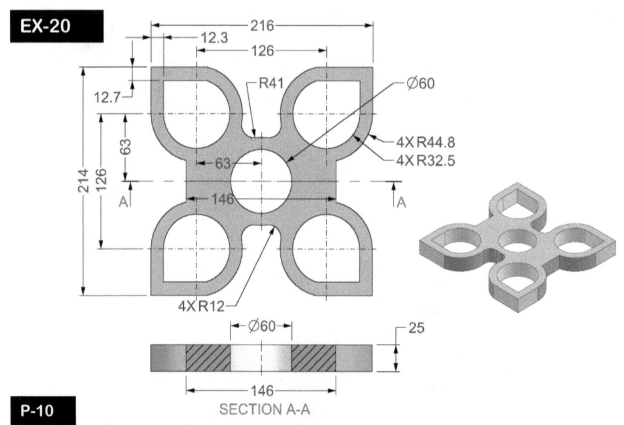

216

12.3

126

R41

Ø60

12.7

4X R44.8

4X R32.5

63

63

214

126

146

A

A

4X R12

Ø60

25

146

SECTION A-A

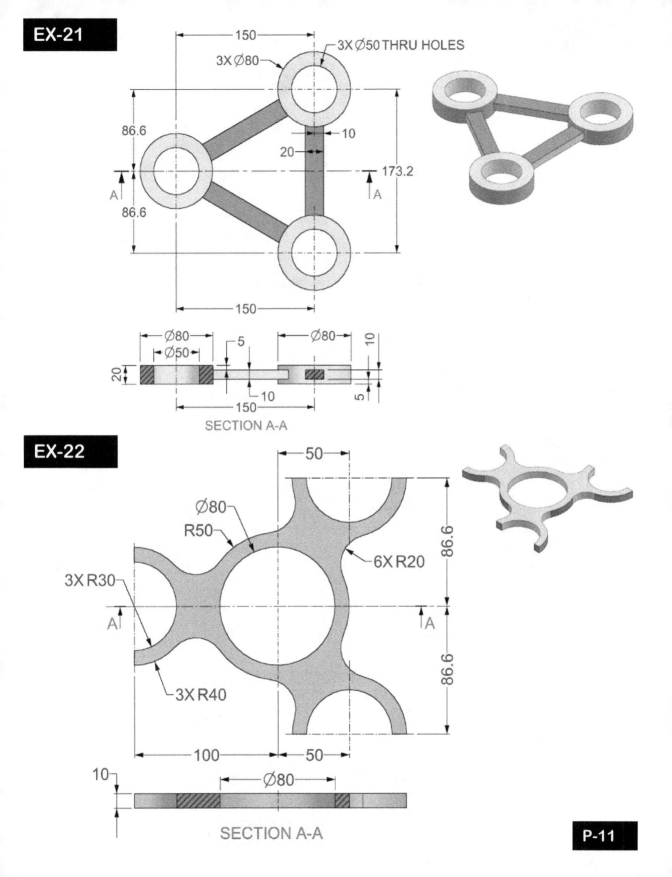

EX-21

150

3X Ø50 THRU HOLES

3X Ø80

86.6

10

20

173.2

A

A

86.6

150

Ø80

Ø50

Ø80

10

20

5

10

5

150

SECTION A-A

EX-22

50

Ø80

R50

86.6

6X R20

3X R30

A

A

86.6

3X R40

100

50

10

Ø80

SECTION A-A

P-11

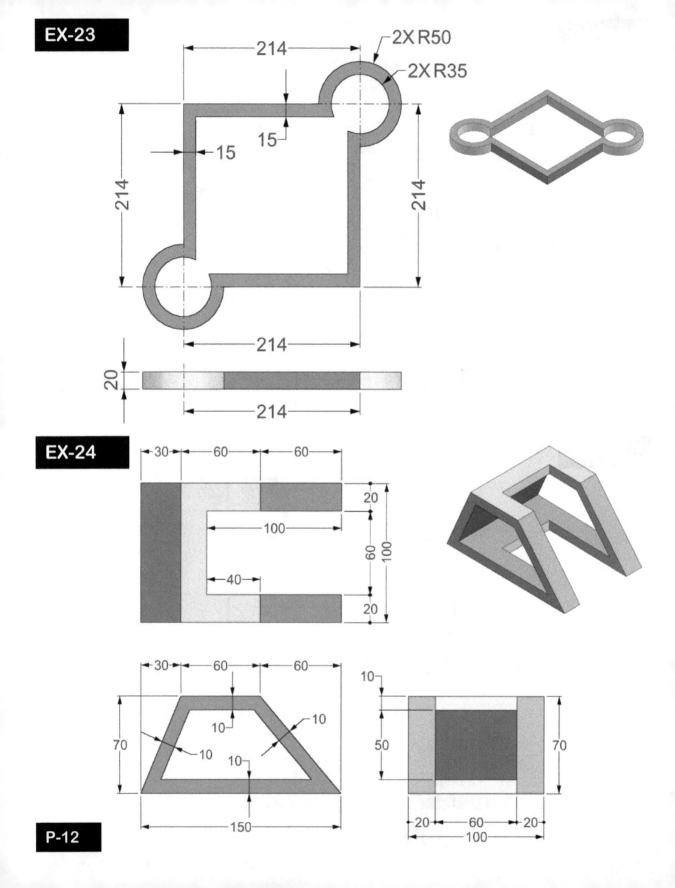

EX-23

214

2X R50

2X R35

15

15

214

214

214

20

214

EX-24

30 · 60 · 60

20

100

60 · 100

40

20

P-12

30 · 60 · 60

10

10

70

10

10

150

10

50

70

20 · 60 · 20

100

EX-25

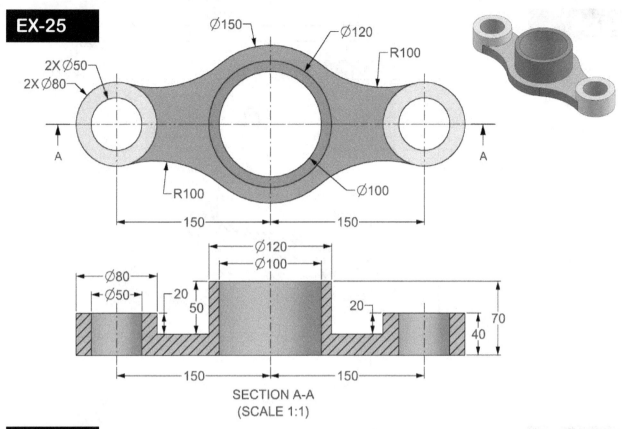

∅150 ∅120 R100

2X ∅50
2X ∅80

R100 ∅100

|←150→|←150→|

∅120
∅100
∅80
∅50

20 50 20

70
40

|←150→|←150→|

SECTION A-A
(SCALE 1:1)

EX-26

∅24 ∅44 ∅36

A   A

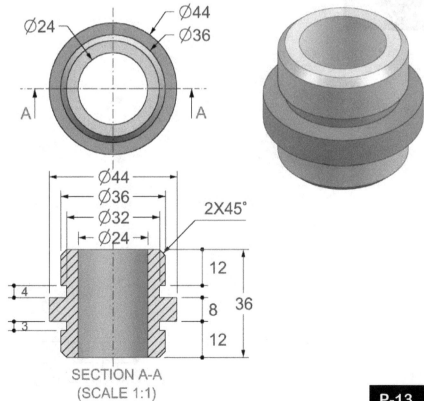

∅44
∅36
∅32
∅24

2X45°

12

4

8   36

3

12

SECTION A-A
(SCALE 1:1)

P-13

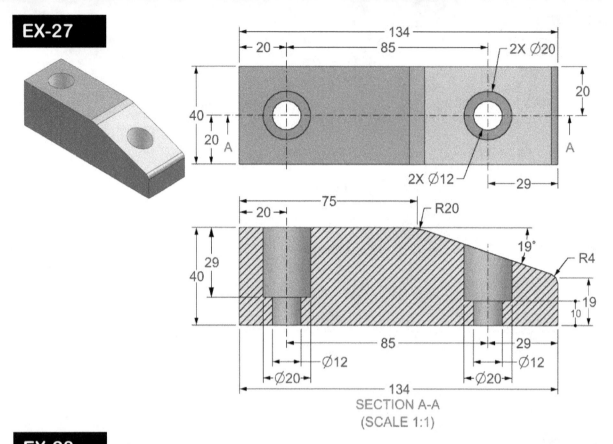

134
20
85
2X Ø20
40
20
20 A
A
2X Ø12
29

75
R20
20
19°
R4
29
40
19
10
85
29
Ø12
Ø12
Ø20
Ø20
134

SECTION A-A
(SCALE 1:1)

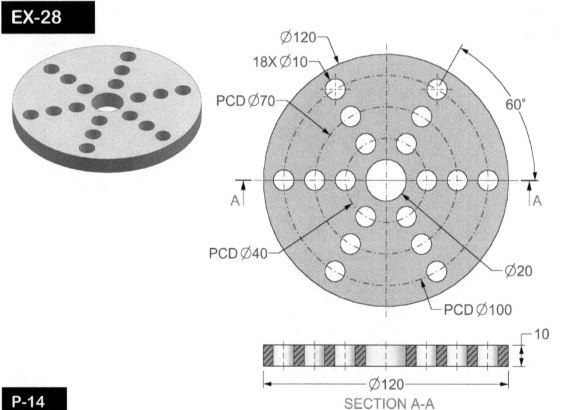

Ø120
18X Ø10
PCD Ø70
60°
PCD Ø40
Ø20
PCD Ø100

10
Ø120
SECTION A-A

EX-29

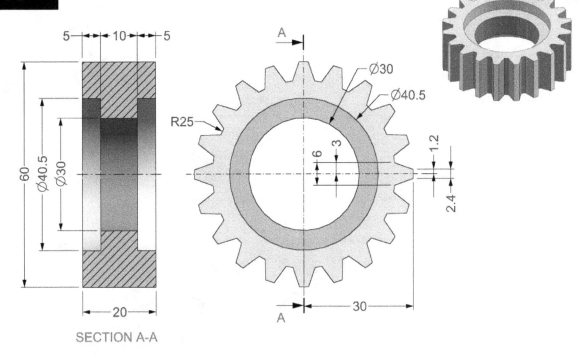

SECTION A-A

5 — 10 — 5

60

Ø40.5

Ø30

20

A

R25

Ø30

Ø40.5

6

3

1.2

2.4

30

A

EX-30

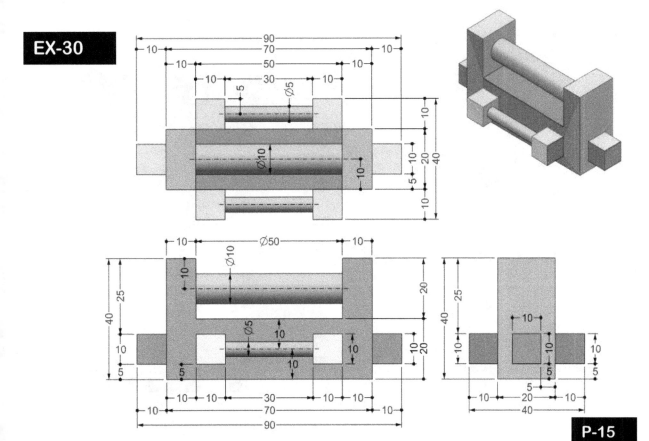

90
70
50
30 Ø5
10
10
10
10
5
10
10
10
20
40
10
5
10

Ø10

10
25
40
10
5

Ø50
Ø10

Ø5
10
10
5
10
10

20
20
10
10

10
10
30
10
10
70
90

40
25
40
10
5

10
10
5
5
10
20
10
40
10

EX-31

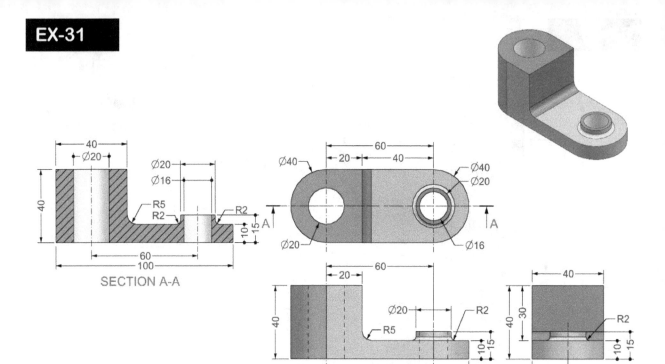

SECTION A-A

EX-32

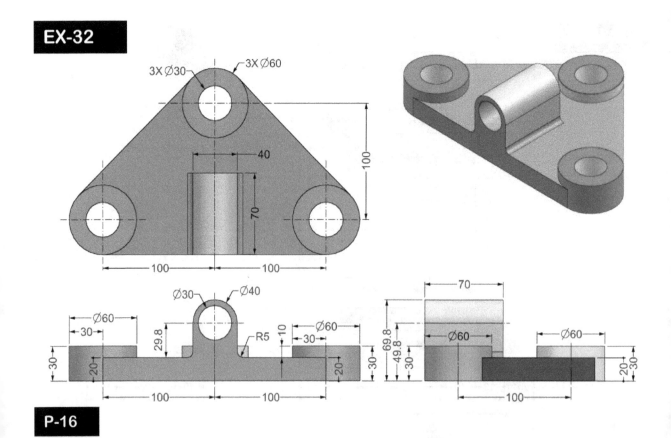

P-16

3X Ø44 3X R35

112.5

30

15

65 65

130

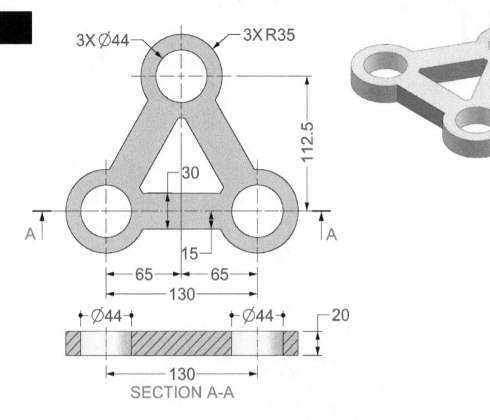

Ø44 Ø44 20

130

SECTION A-A

20 80 15 x 45°

30

45

120 Ø60 15 15

R15 15

45

20 45 35

20

20

100 80

R10

20

15

100

20 x 45° 60 23

20

R30

2X ⌴ Ø16 ↧8 2X Ø12 THRU ALL

20

74 33

Ø30 53

20 20

15 30 15 15 30 15 100

120

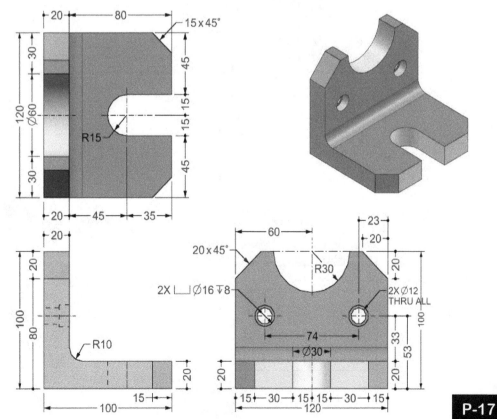

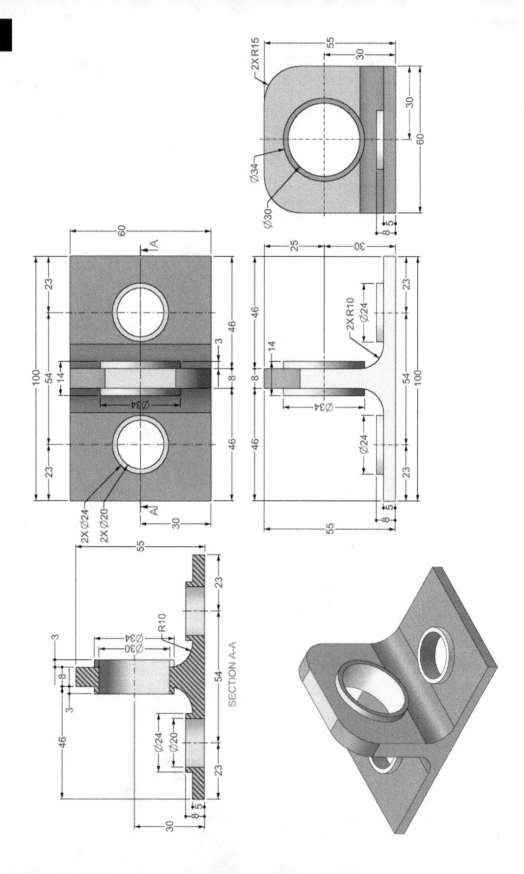

SECTION A-A

EX-36

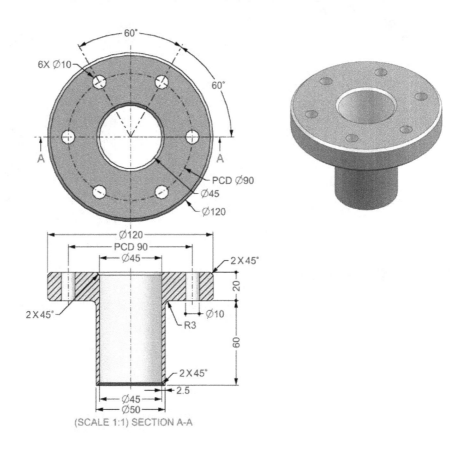

60°

6X Ø10

60°

PCD Ø90
Ø45
Ø120

Ø120
PCD 90
Ø45
2 X 45°
20
2 X 45°
Ø10
R3
60
2 X 45°
2.5
Ø45
Ø50

(SCALE 1:1) SECTION A-A

EX-37

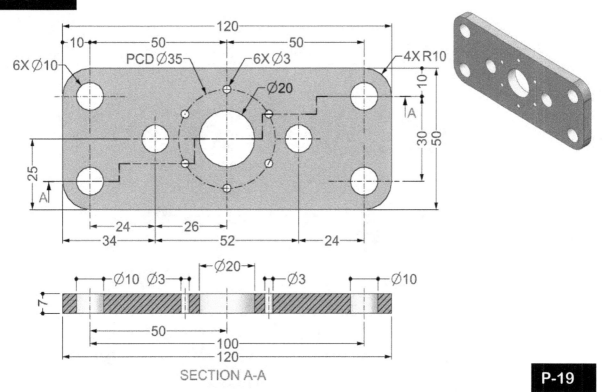

120
10
50
50
6X Ø10
PCD Ø35
6X Ø3
4X R10
Ø20
10
A
30
50
25
A
24
26
34
52
24

Ø10 Ø3
Ø20
Ø3
Ø10
7
50
100
120

SECTION A-A

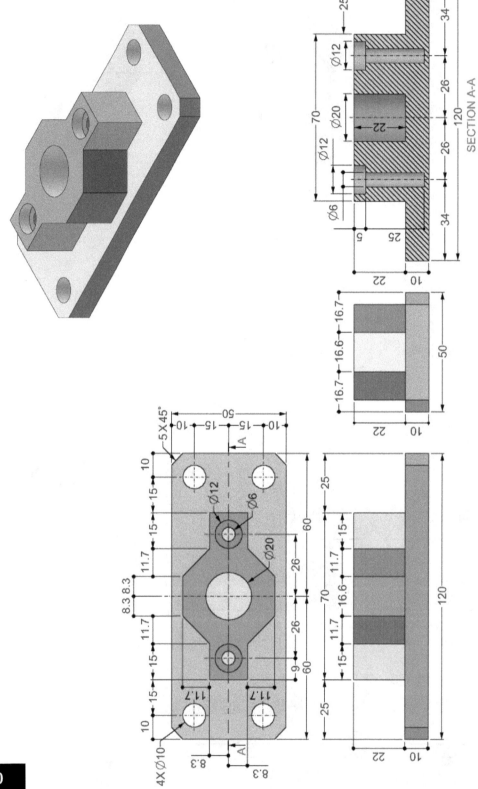

SECTION A-A

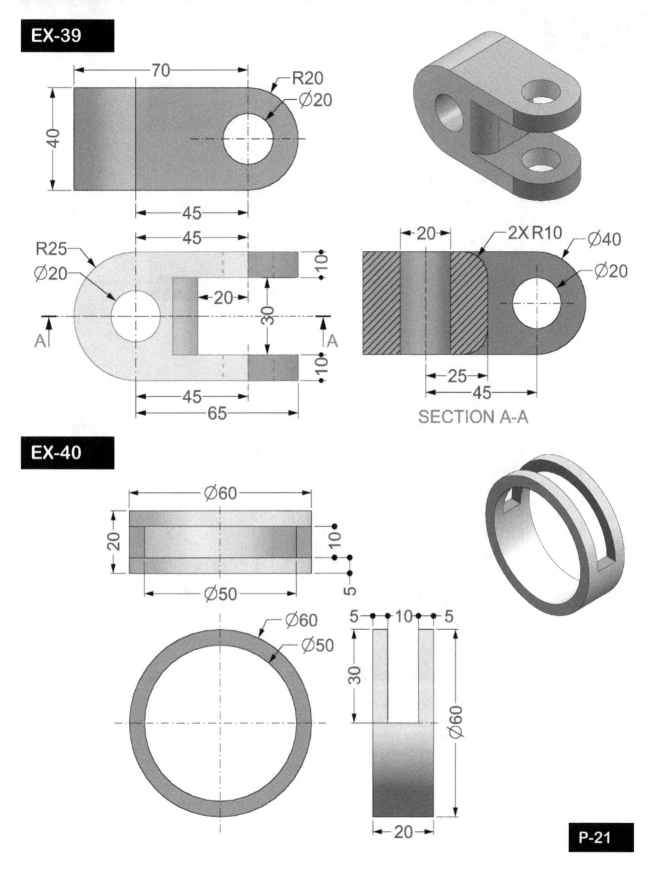

EX-39

70
R20
Ø20
40
45

R25
Ø20
45
20
30
10
10
45
65
A — A

20
2X R10
Ø40
Ø20
25
45
SECTION A-A

EX-40

Ø60
20
10
5
Ø50

Ø60
Ø50

5 — 10 — 5
30
Ø60
20

P-21

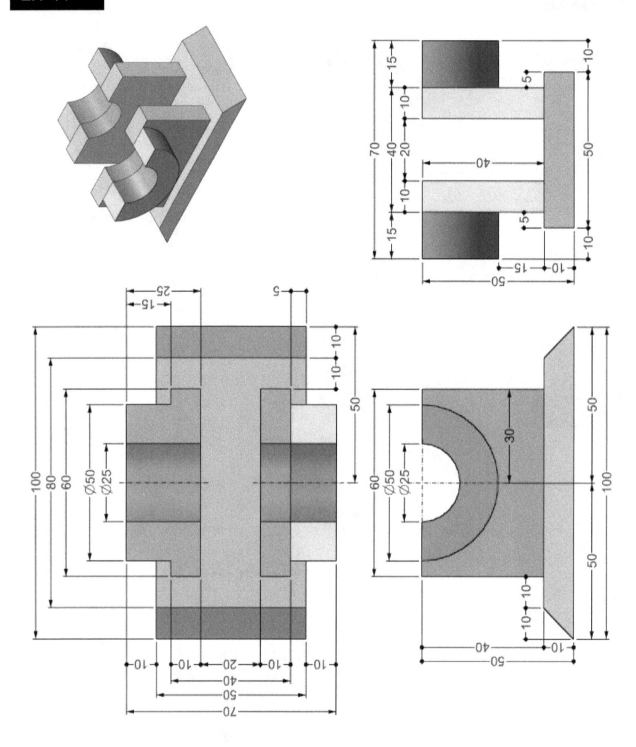

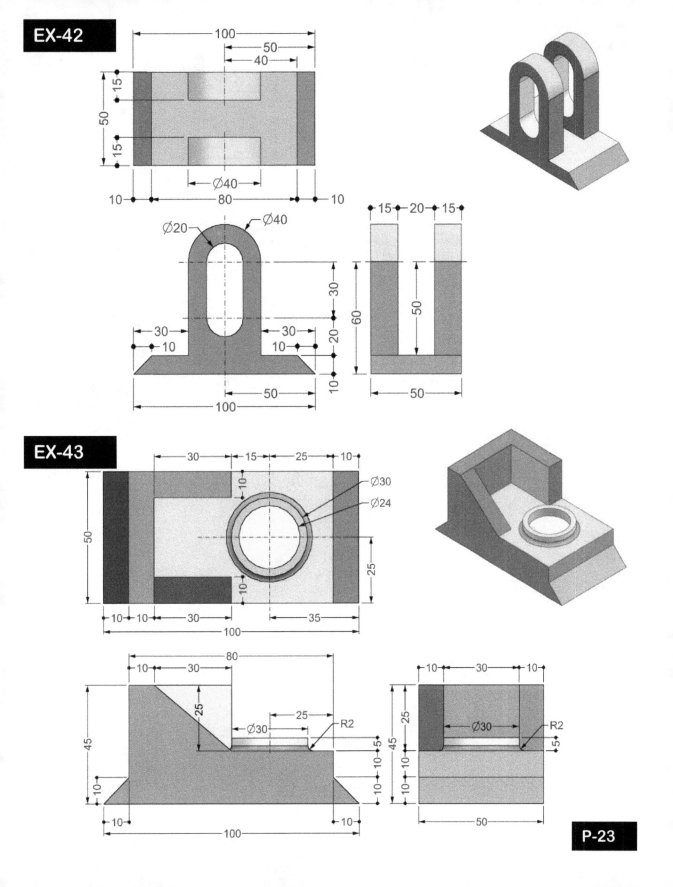

EX-42

EX-43

P-23

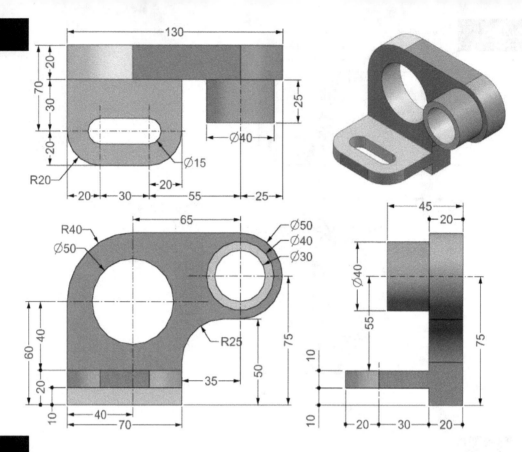

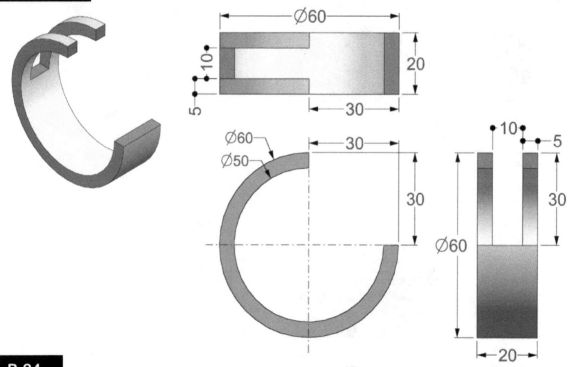

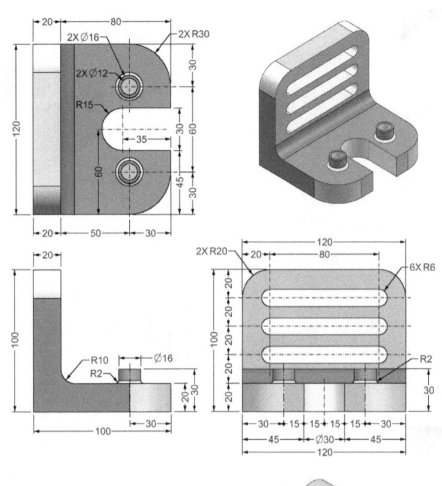

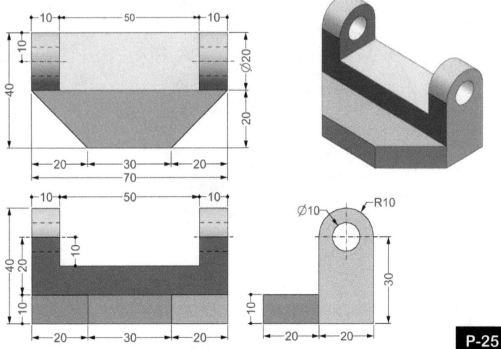

EX-48

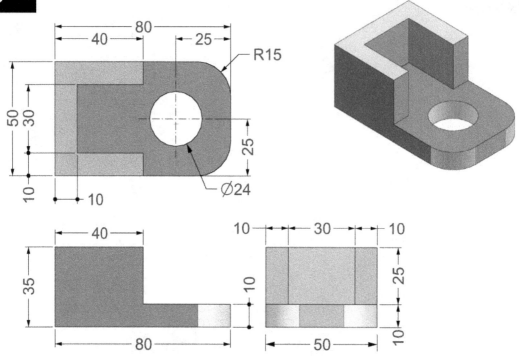

EX-49

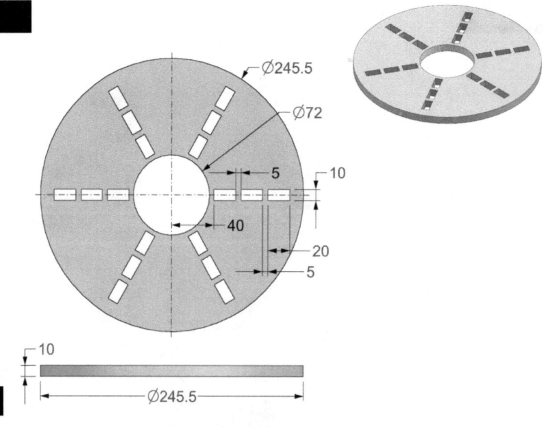

P-26

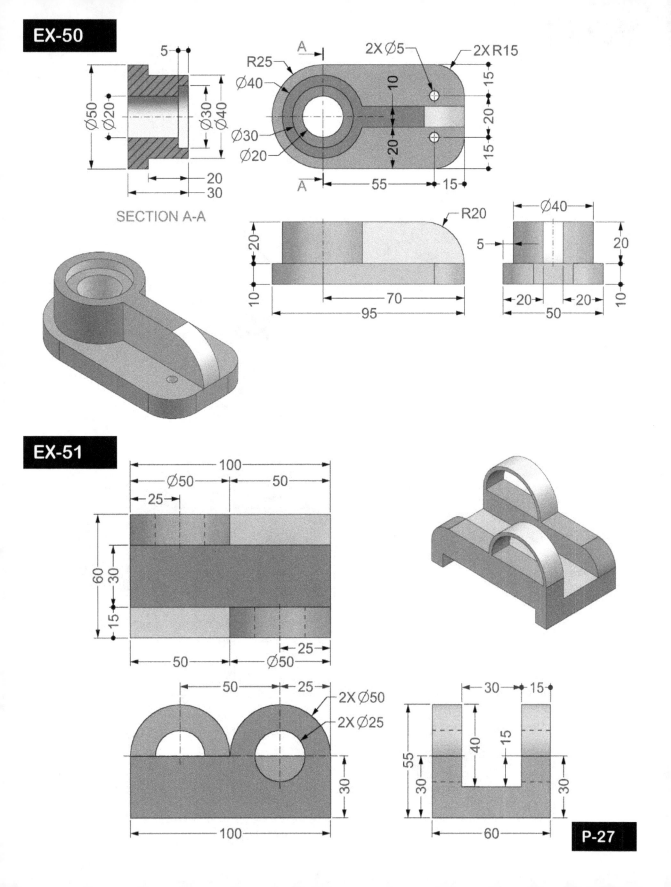

EX-50

SECTION A-A

5
Ø50
Ø20
Ø30
Ø40
20
30

A
R25
Ø40
Ø30
Ø20
2X Ø5
2X R15
10
20
15
20
15
55
15

R20
20
10
70
95

Ø40
5
20
20
50
10
20

EX-51

100
Ø50
50
25
60
30
15
50
Ø50
25

2X Ø50
2X Ø25
50
25
30
100

30
15
55
40
15
30
30
60

P-27

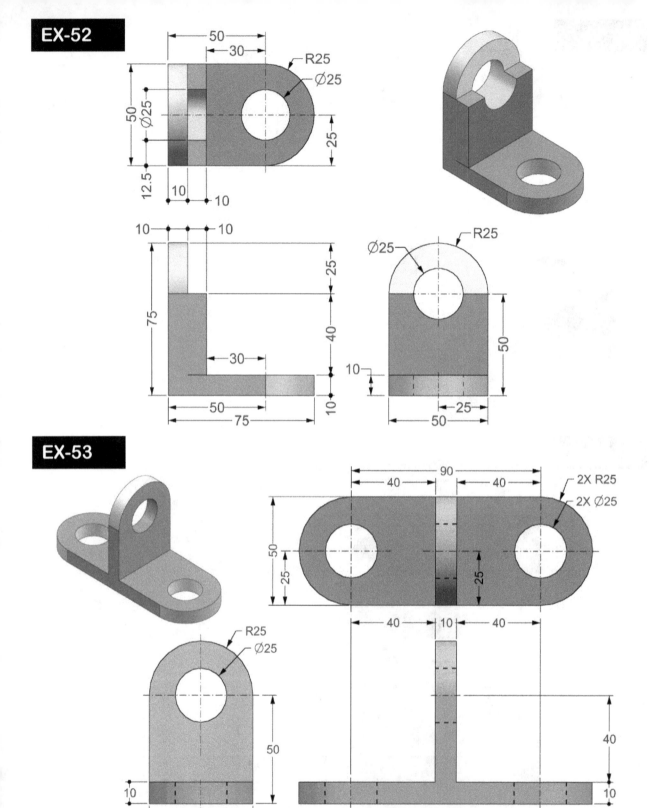

EX-52

EX-53

P-28

EX-54

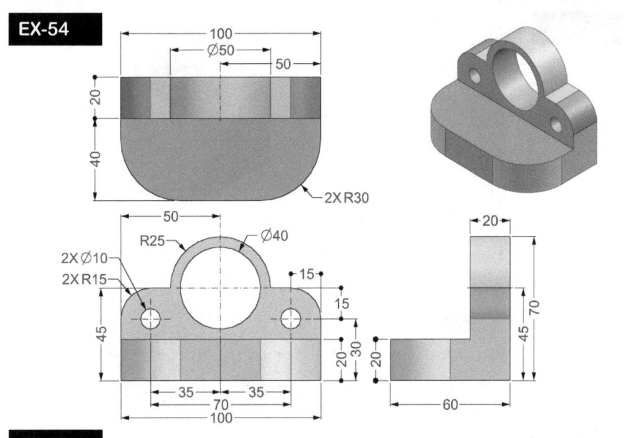

100
Ø50
50
20
40
2X R30

50
R25
Ø40
2X Ø10
2X R15
15
15
45
20
30
35
35
20
70
100
20
70
45
20
60

EX-55

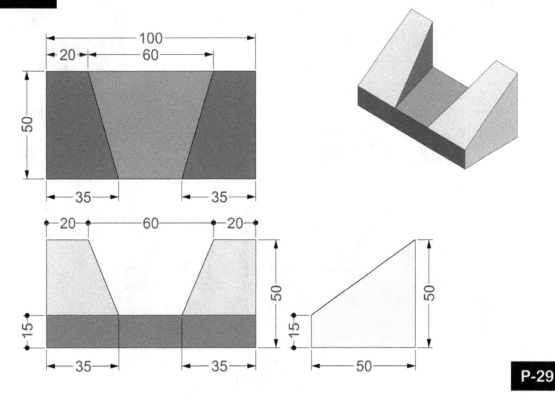

100
20
60
50
35
35

20
60
20
50
15
35
35

50
15
50

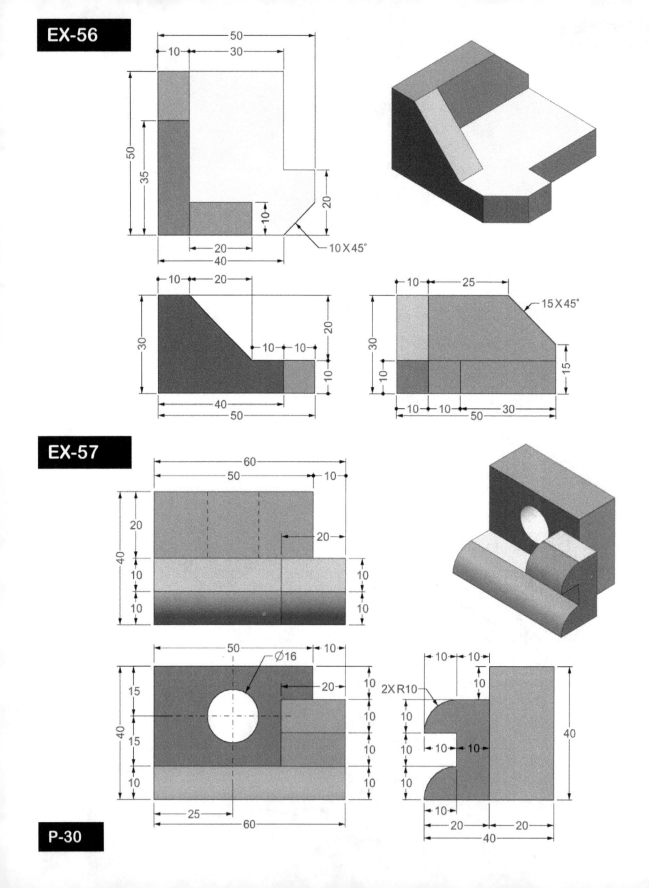

EX-56

50
10 · 30
50
35
20
10
20
40
10 X 45°

10 · 20
30
20
10 · 10
10
40
50

10 · 25
15 X 45°
30
10
15
10 · 10
50 · 30

EX-57

60
50 · 10
20
20
40
10
10
10
10

50 · ∅16 · 10
15
20 · 10
40
10
15
10
25
60
10

10 · 10
10
2 X R10
10
10 · 10
10
40
10
20 · 20
40

P-30

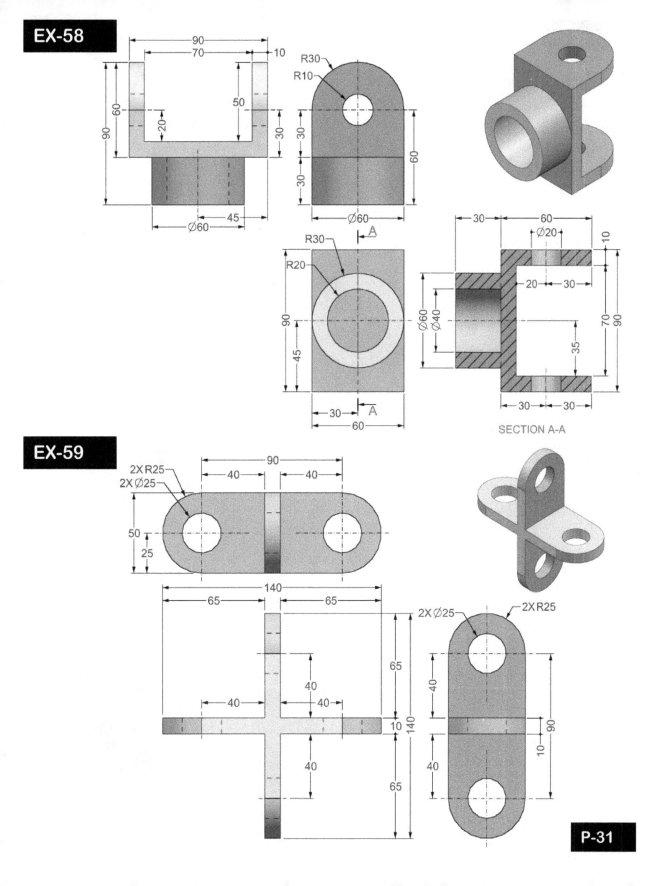

EX-58

R30
R10
R30
R20

Ø60

SECTION A-A

EX-59

2X R25
2X Ø25

2X Ø25
2X R25

P-31

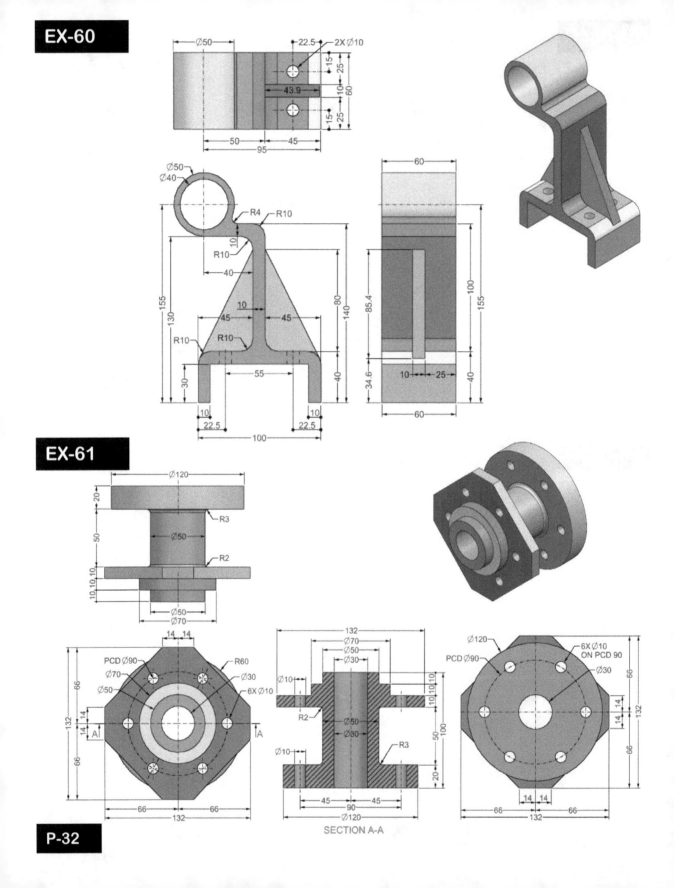

EX-60

EX-61

P-32

SECTION A-A

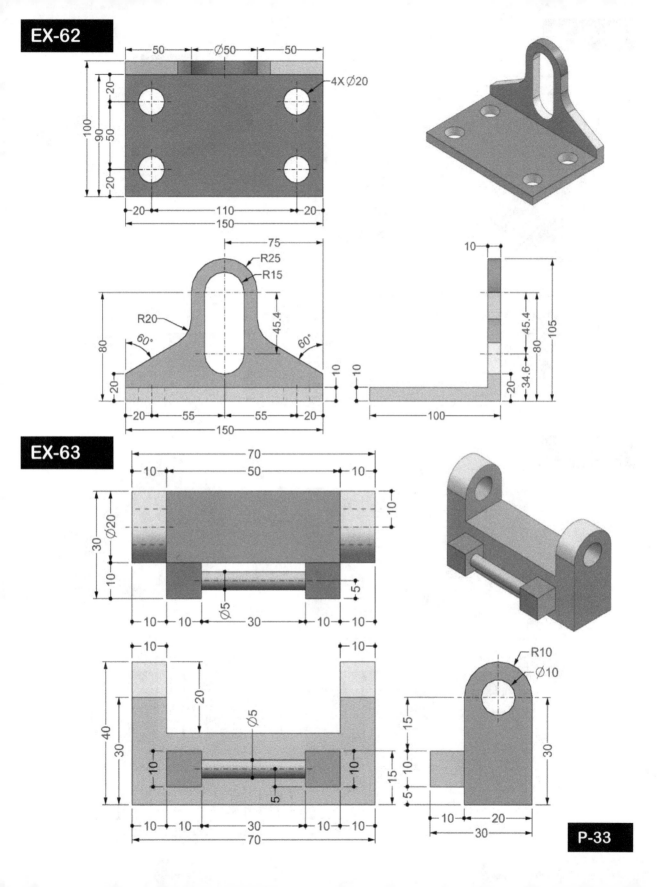

EX-62

EX-63

P-33

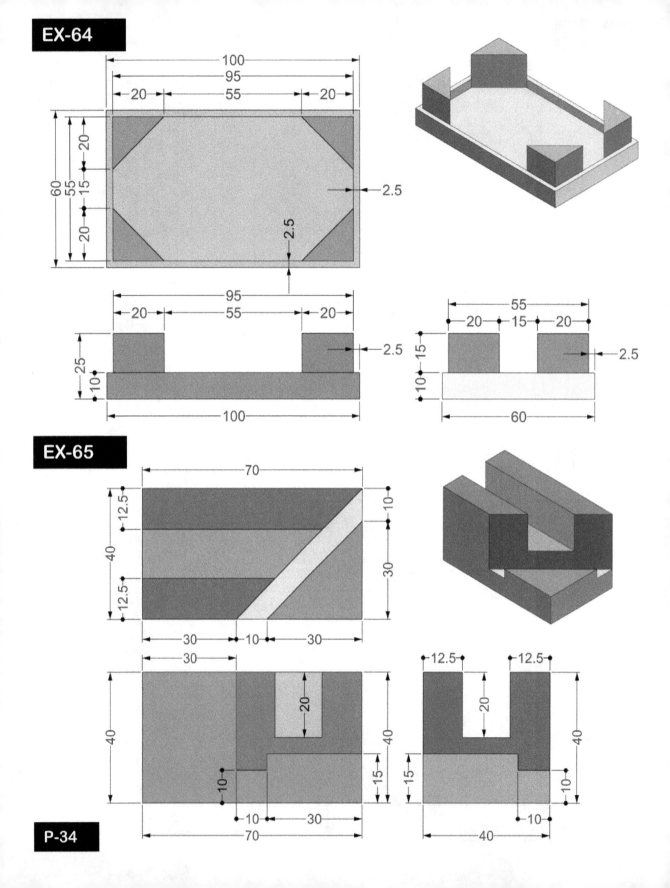

EX-64

EX-65

P-34

EX-66

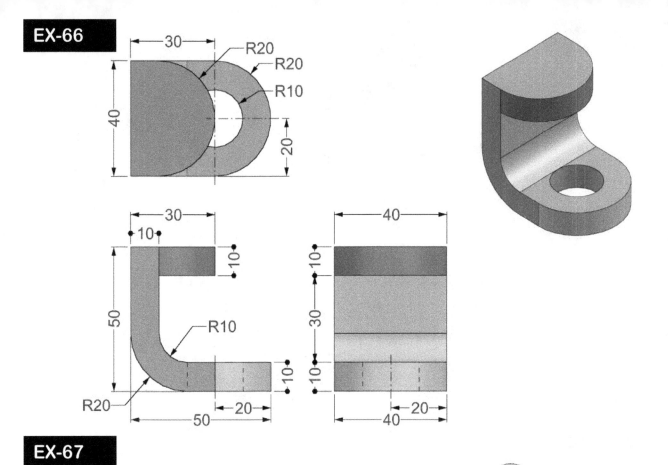

EX-67

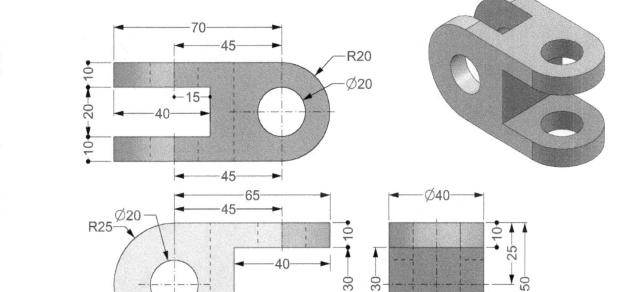

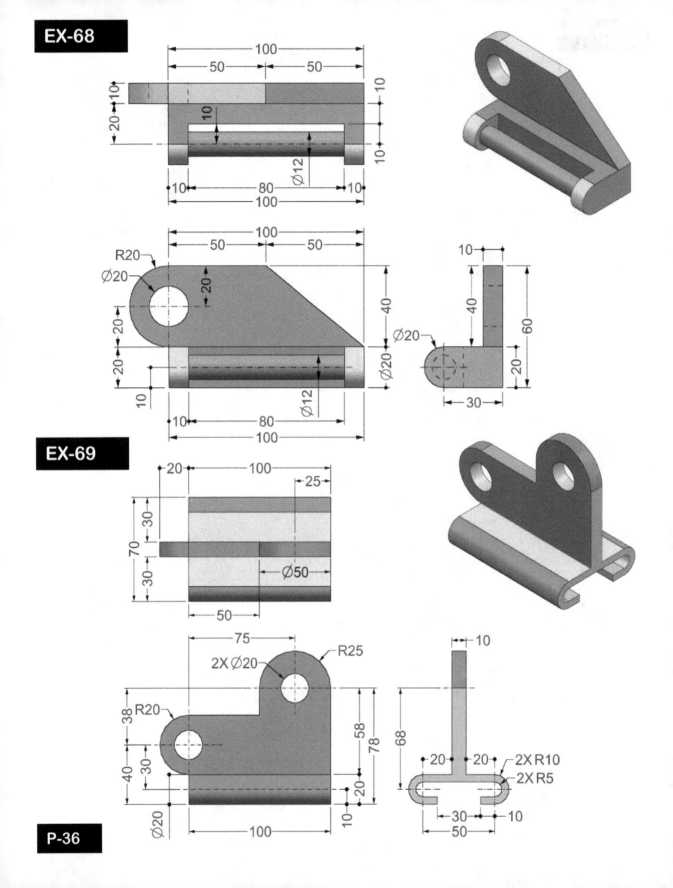

EX-68

EX-69

P-36

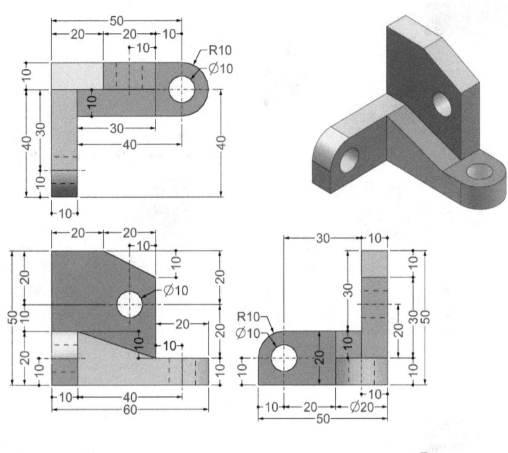

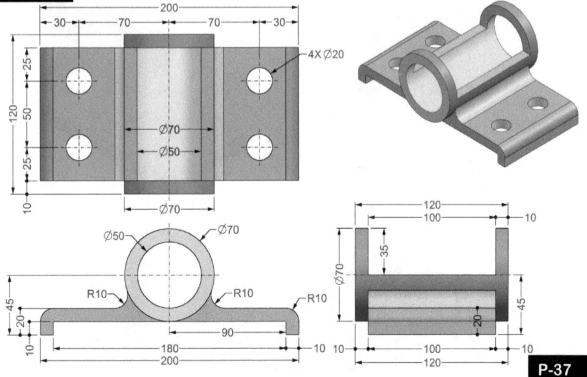

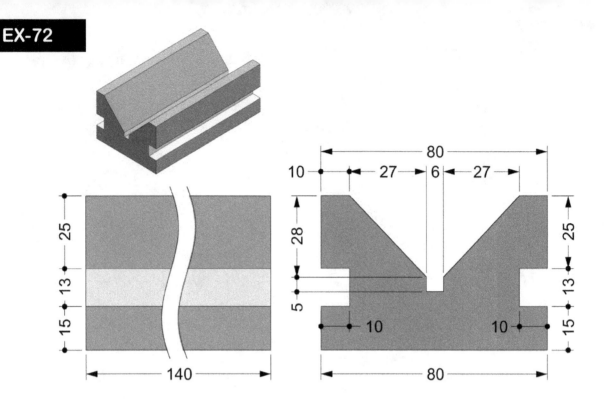

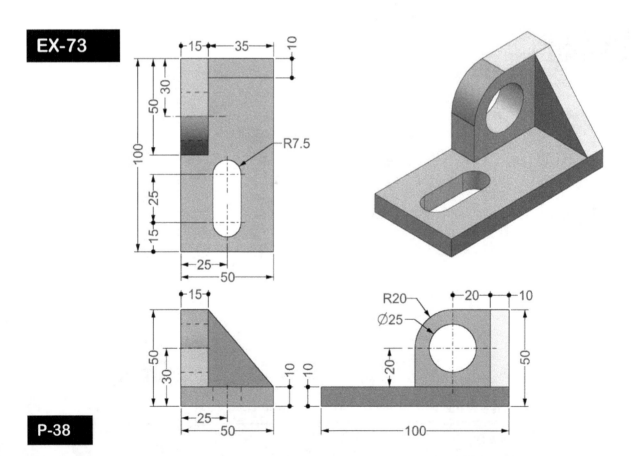

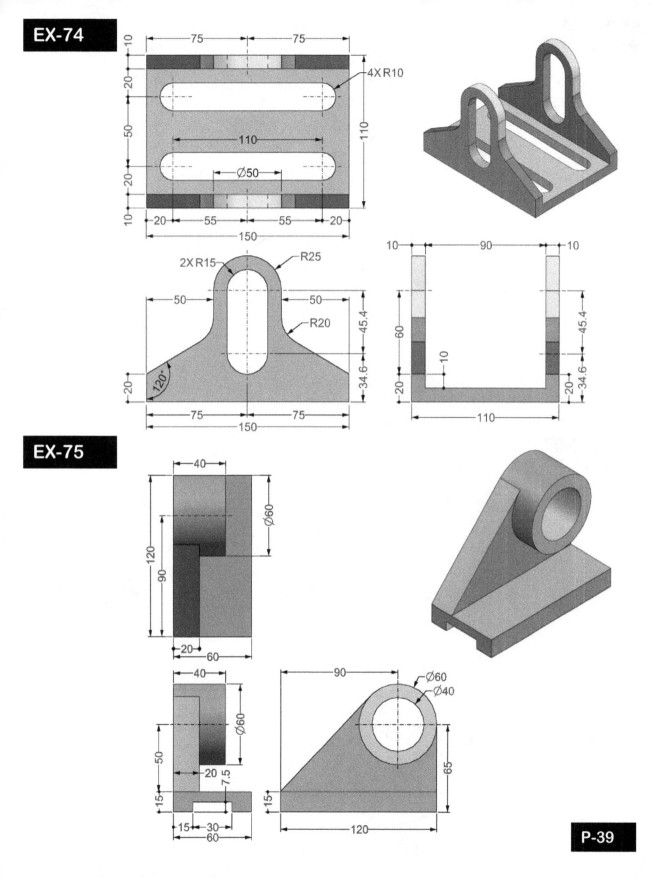

EX-74

75 75
10
4X R10
20
50
110
110
20
10
20 55 55 20
150

2X R15 R25
50 50
R20
45.4
34.6
20 120°
75 75
150

10 90 10
60 45.4
10
20 34.6
110

EX-75

40
Ø60
120
90
20
60

40
Ø60
50
20
7.5
15
15 30
60

90
Ø60
Ø40
65
15
120

P-39

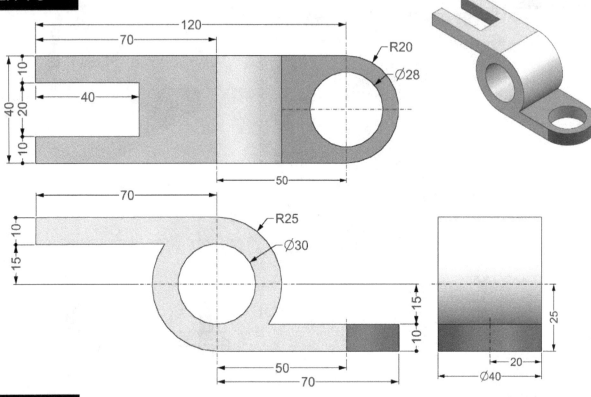

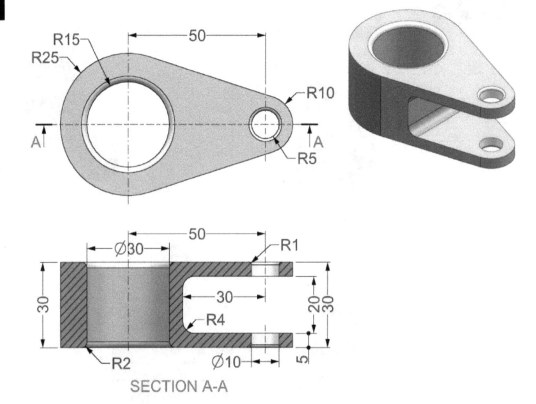

SECTION A-A

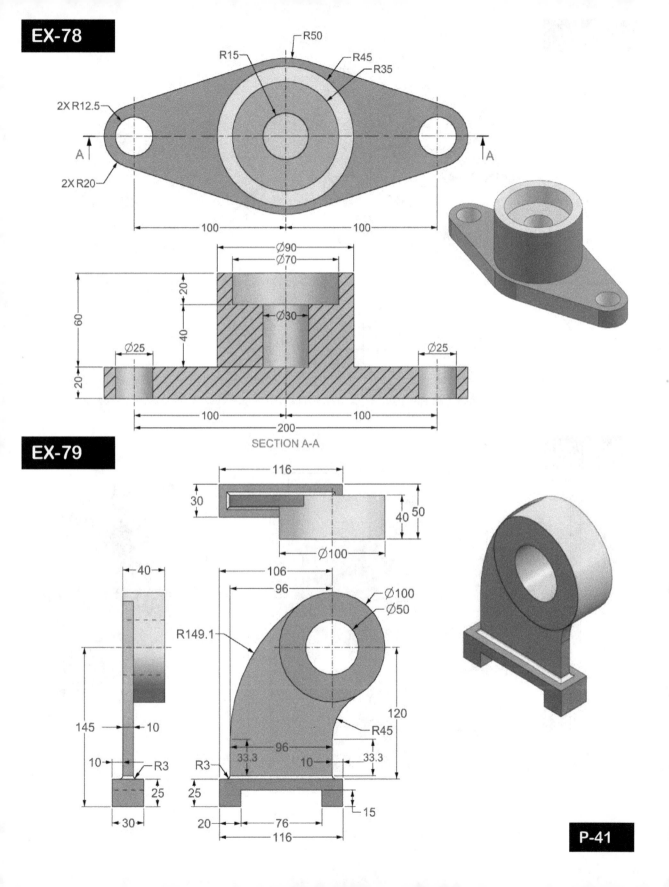

EX-78

R50
R15
R45
R35
2X R12.5
2X R20
A
A
100
100

Ø90
Ø70
20
60
40
Ø30
Ø25
Ø25
20
100
100
200
SECTION A-A

EX-79

116
30
40 50
Ø100

40
106
96
Ø100
Ø50
R149.1
145
10
120
R45
10
R3
R3
33.3
96
10
33.3
25
25
30
20
76
15
116

P-41

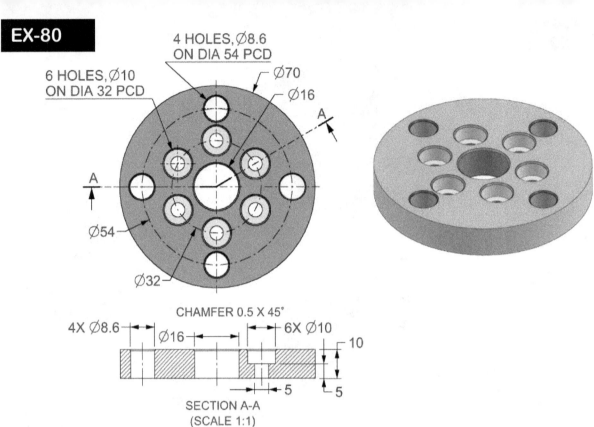

4 HOLES, Ø8.6
ON DIA 54 PCD

6 HOLES, Ø10
ON DIA 32 PCD

Ø70

Ø16

A

A

Ø54

Ø32

CHAMFER 0.5 X 45°

4X Ø8.6   Ø16   6X Ø10

10

5

5

SECTION A-A
(SCALE 1:1)

EX-81

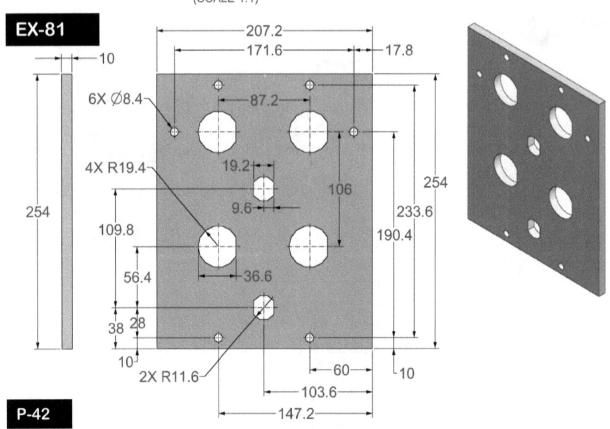

207.2

171.6   17.8

10

6X Ø8.4

87.2

4X R19.4

19.2

106

254

9.6

233.6

109.8

190.4

56.4   36.6

254

38   28

10

60   10

2X R11.6

103.6

147.2

EX-82

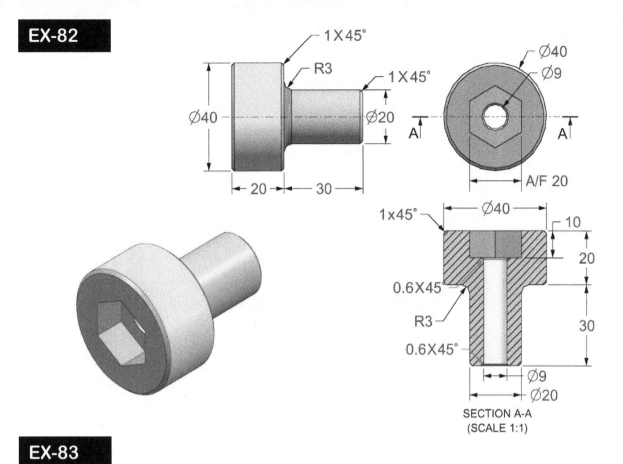

1 X 45°
R3
1 X 45°
Ø40
Ø20
20
30

Ø40
Ø9
A/F 20

1x45°
Ø40
10
20
0.6X45°
R3
30
0.6X45°
Ø9
Ø20

SECTION A-A
(SCALE 1:1)

EX-83

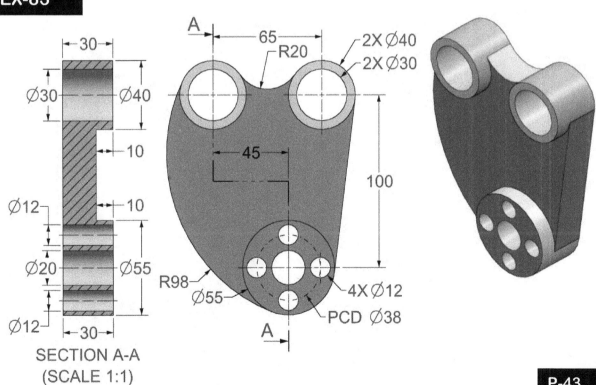

30
Ø30
Ø40
10
10
Ø12
Ø20
Ø55
Ø12
30

SECTION A-A
(SCALE 1:1)

A
65
R20
2X Ø40
2X Ø30
45
100
R98
Ø55
4X Ø12
PCD Ø38
A

EX-84

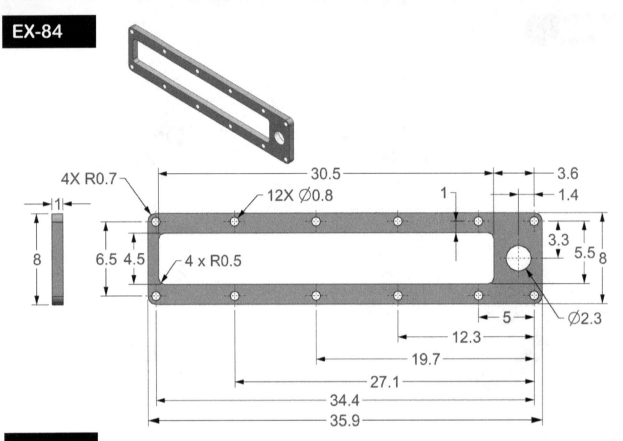

4X R0.7
12X Ø0.8
4 x R0.5
30.5
3.6
1.4
1
3.3
5.5
8
8
6.5
4.5
1
Ø2.3
5
12.3
19.7
27.1
34.4
35.9

EX-85

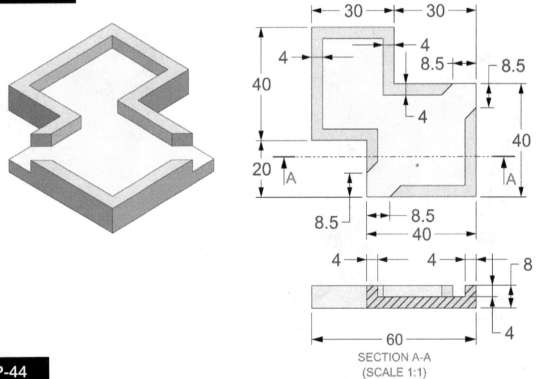

30
30
4
4
8.5
8.5
40
4
40
20
A
A
8.5
8.5
40
4
4
8
60
4
8.5
SECTION A-A
(SCALE 1:1)

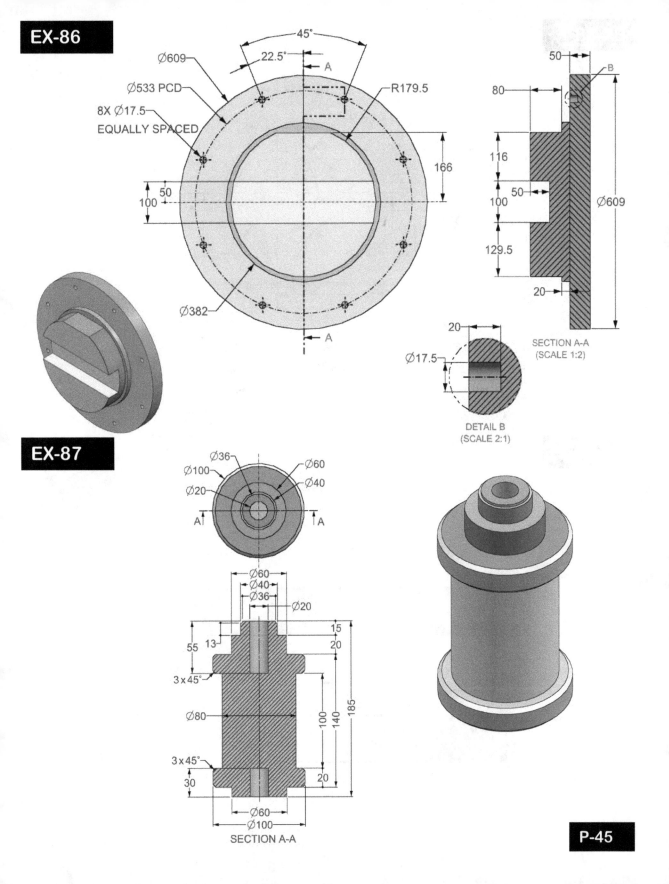

EX-86

Ø609
Ø533 PCD
8X Ø17.5
EQUALLY SPACED
45°
22.5°
A
R179.5
166
50
100
Ø382
A

50
80
116
50
100
129.5
20
Ø609
B
SECTION A-A
(SCALE 1:2)

20
Ø17.5
DETAIL B
(SCALE 2:1)

EX-87

Ø36
Ø100
Ø20
Ø60
Ø40
A
A

Ø60
Ø40
Ø36
Ø20
15
20
55
13
3 x 45°
Ø80
100
140
185
3 x 45°
30
20
Ø60
Ø100
SECTION A-A

P-45

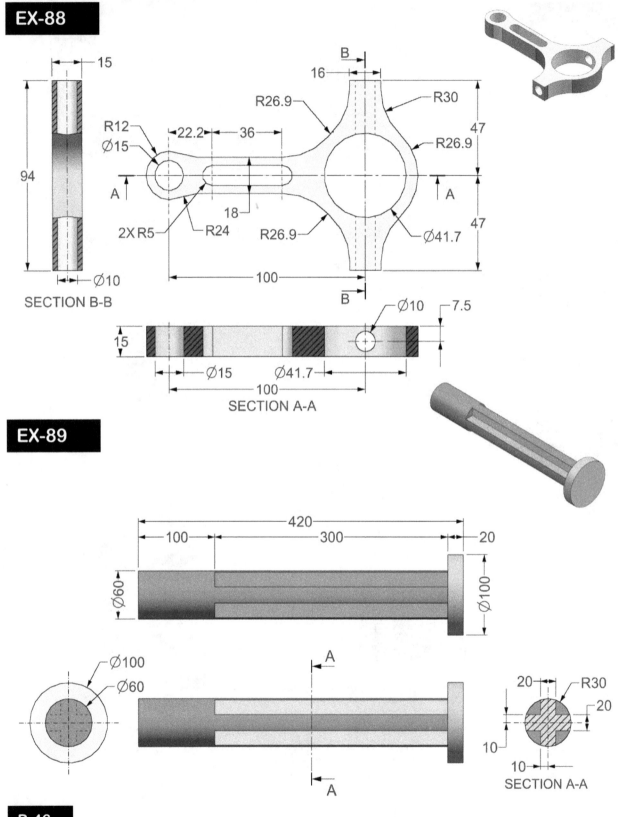

EX-88

15

94

Ø10

SECTION B-B

R12
Ø15

22.2

36

18

2X R5

R24

B

16

R26.9

R30

47

R26.9

47

R26.9

Ø41.7

100

B

15

Ø10

7.5

Ø15

Ø41.7

100

SECTION A-A

EX-89

420

100

300

20

Ø60

Ø100

Ø100

Ø60

A

A

20

R30

20

10

10

SECTION A-A

P-46

EX-90

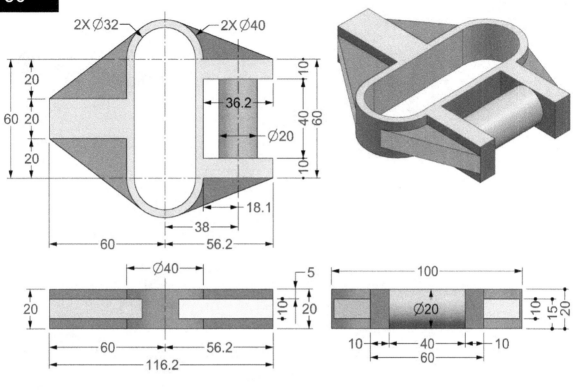

EX-91

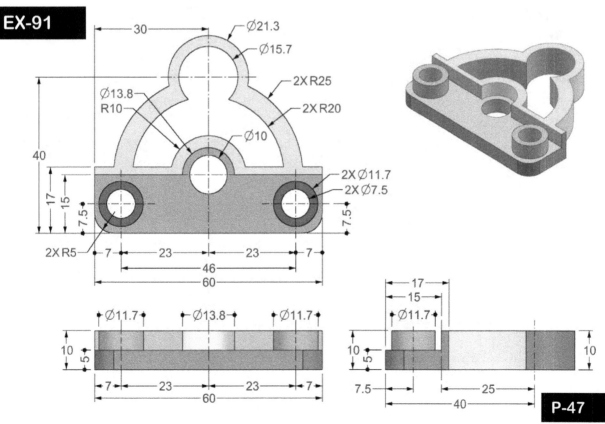

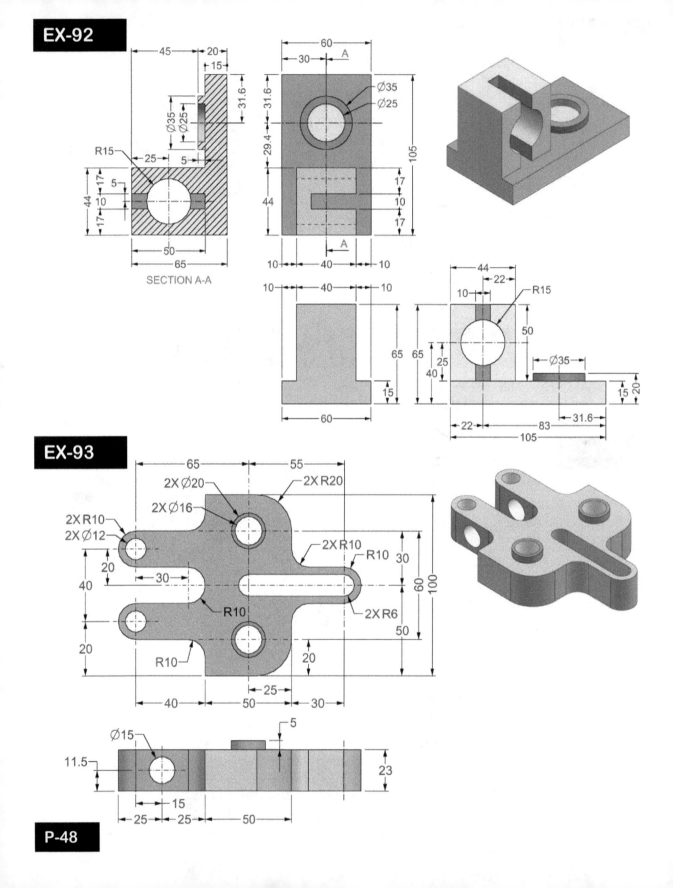

EX-92

45 · 20
15
Ø35 · Ø25
31.6
R15
25 · 5
17
5
44 · 10
17
50
65
SECTION A-A

60
30 · A
31.6
Ø35
Ø25
29.4
105
44
17
10
17
A
10 · 40 · 10

10 · 40 · 10
65
15
60

44
22
10 · R15
50
Ø35
65 · 25
40
15 · 20
22 · 83 · 31.6
105

EX-93

65 · 55
2X Ø20 · 2X R20
2X Ø16
2X R10
2X Ø12
2X R10
R10 · 30
20
40 · 30 · 60 · 100
R10
20 · 2X R6
50
20
R10
25
40 · 50 · 30

5
Ø15
11.5
23
15
25 · 25 · 50

P-48

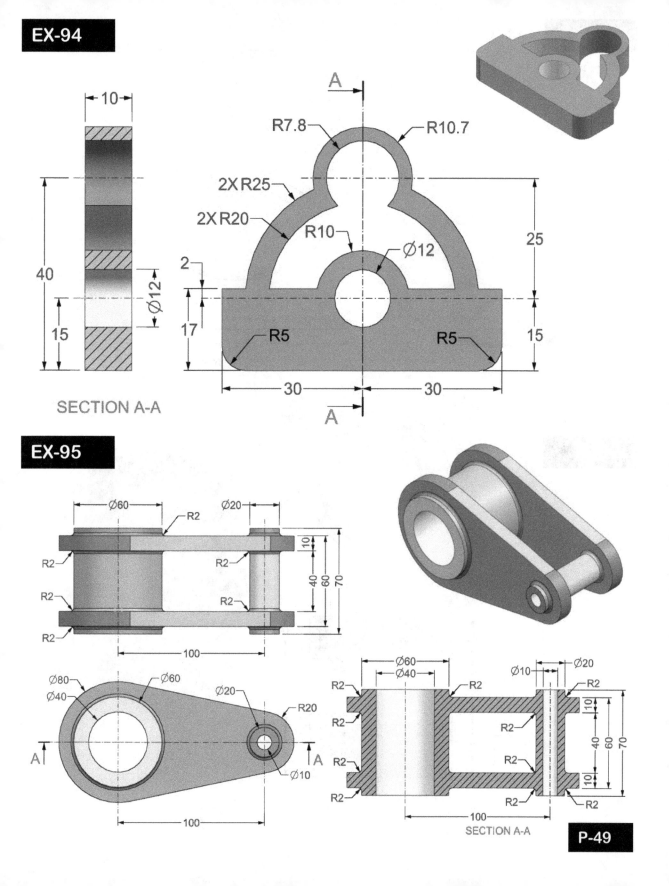

EX-94

SECTION A-A

10

40

15

Ø12

2XR25
2XR20
R7.8
R10.7
R10
Ø12
2
17
R5
R5
25
15
30
30
A
A

EX-95

Ø60
R2
Ø20
R2
R2
R2
R2
10
40
60
70
100

Ø80
Ø40
Ø60
Ø20
R20
A
A
Ø10
100

Ø60
Ø40
R2
Ø10
Ø20
R2
R2
R2
R2
R2
R2
R2
R2
10
40
60
70
10
100

SECTION A-A

P-49

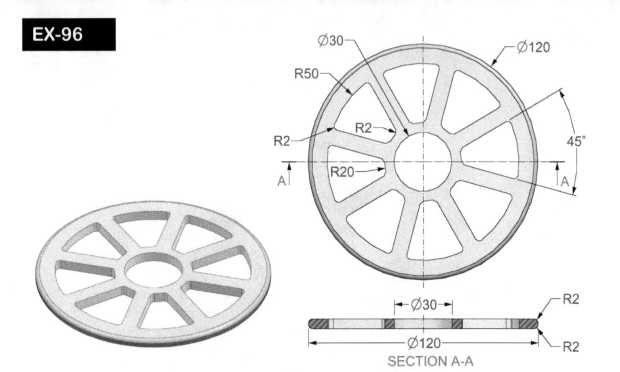

Ø30
R50
Ø120
R2
R2
R2
R20
45°
A
A

Ø30
R2
Ø120
R2
SECTION A-A

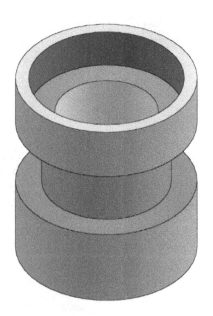

Ø70
Ø60
Ø40
A
A

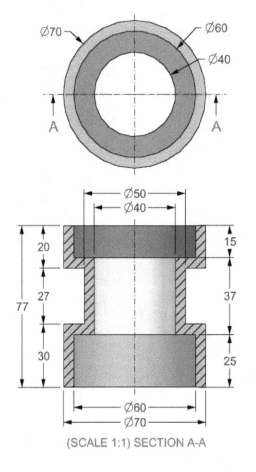

Ø50
Ø40
20
15
27
37
77
30
25
Ø60
Ø70
(SCALE 1:1) SECTION A-A

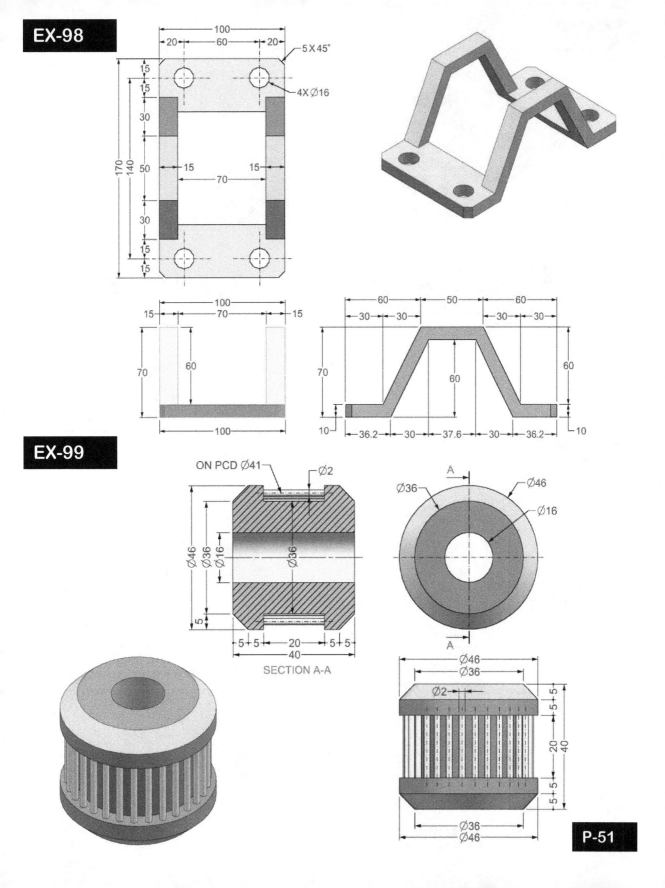

EX-98

100
20 60 20
5 X 45°
15
15
4X Ø16
30
15 15
50
70
30
15
15

170
140

100
15 70 15
70
60
100

60 50 60
30 30 30 30
70
60
60
10 36.2 30 37.6 30 36.2 10

EX-99

ON PCD Ø41
Ø2
A
Ø36
Ø46
Ø16
Ø46
Ø36
Ø16
Ø36
A
5
5 5 20 5 5
40
SECTION A-A

Ø46
Ø36
Ø2
5 5
20 40
5 5
5
Ø36
Ø46

P-51

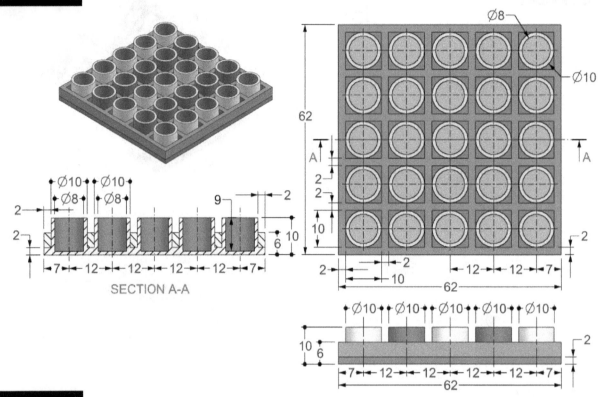

SECTION A-A

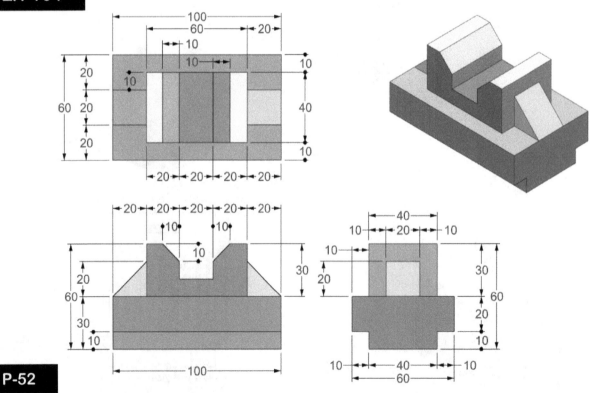

EX-102

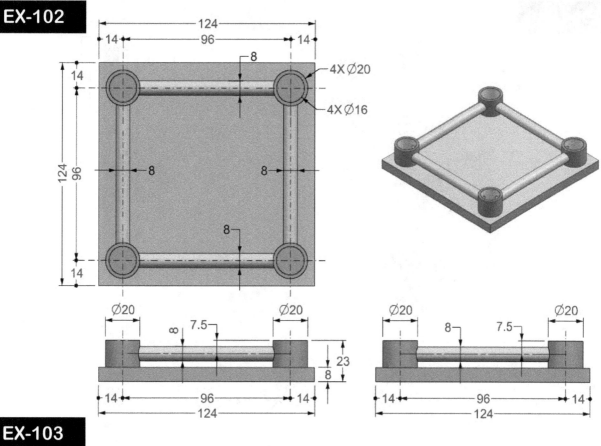

EX-103

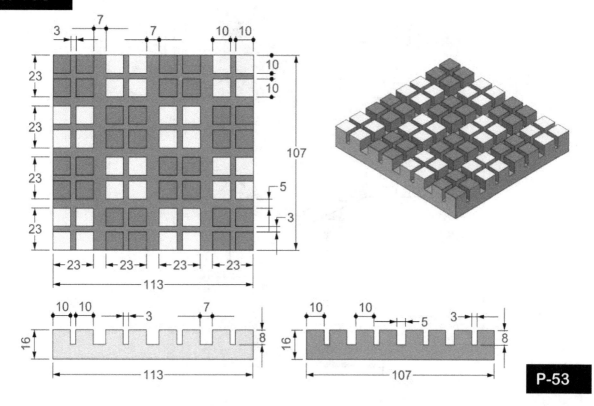

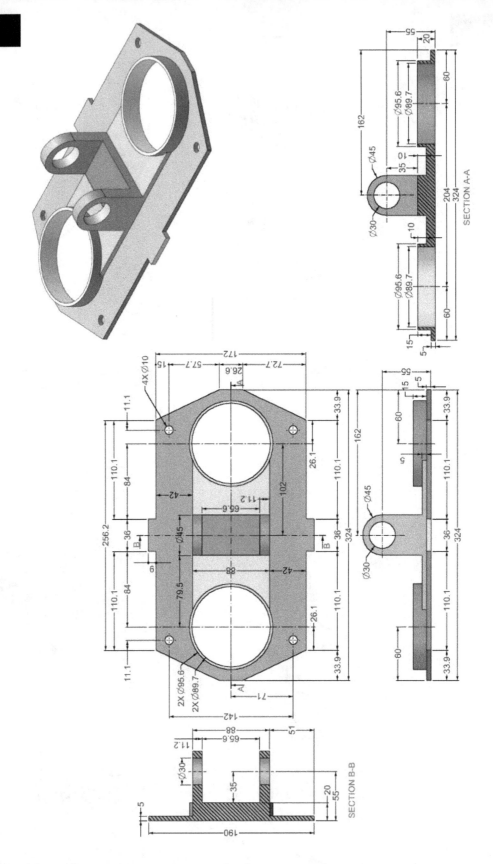

SECTION A-A

SECTION B-B

EX-105

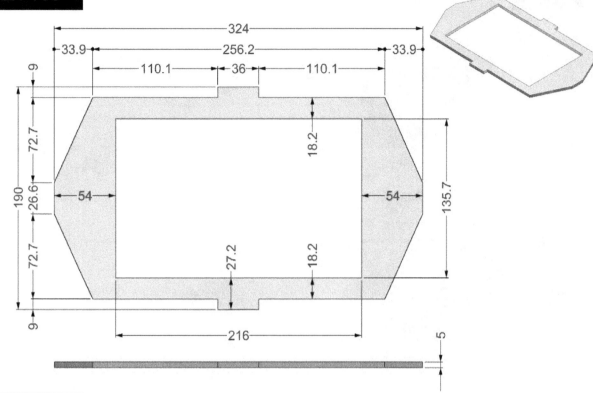

EX-106

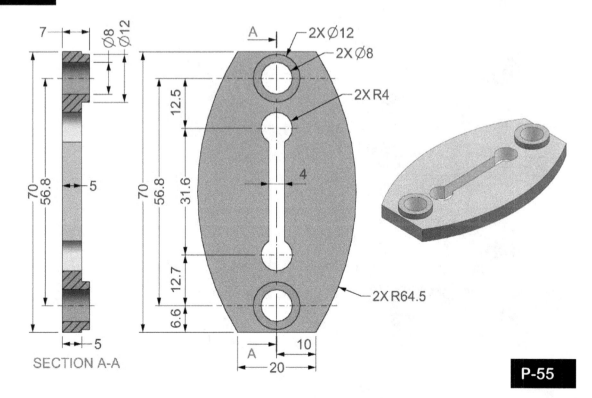

SECTION A-A

EX-107

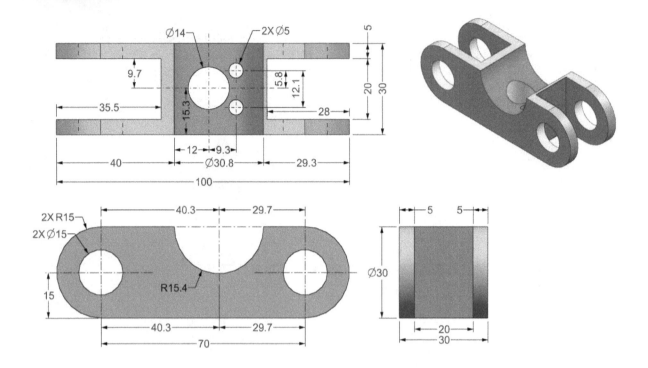

EX-108

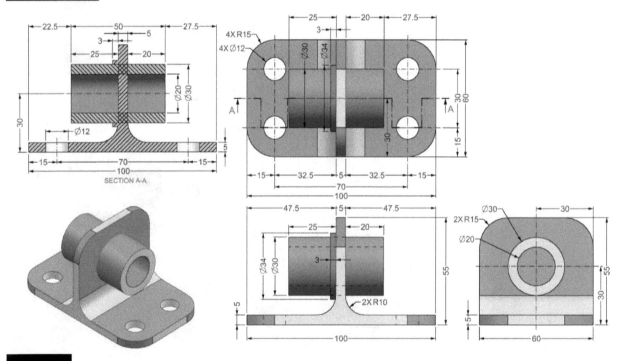

SECTION A-A

P-56

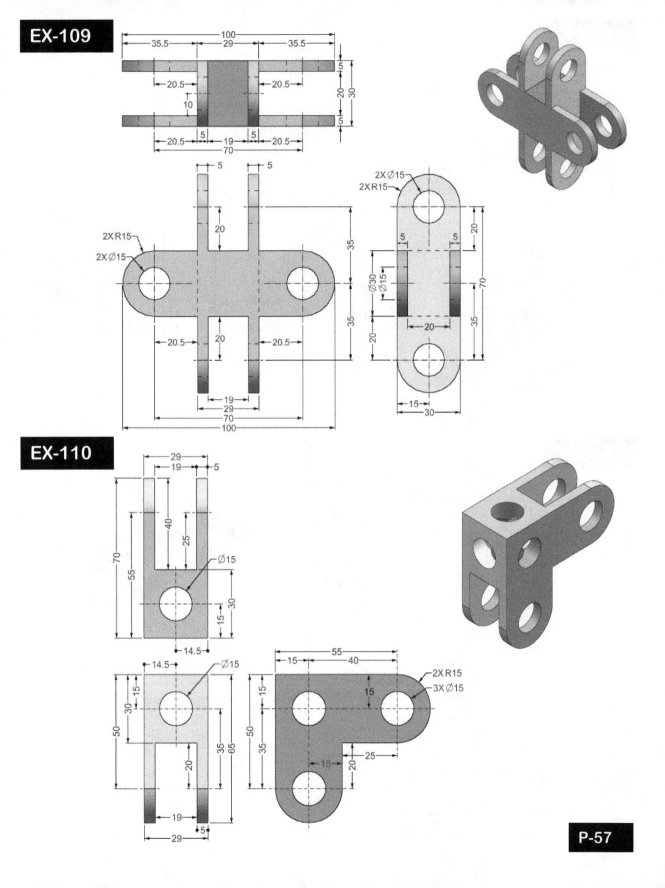

EX-109

EX-110

P-57

EX-111

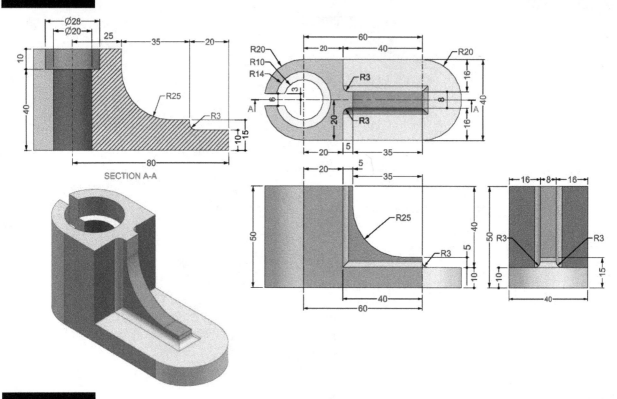

SECTION A-A

EX-112

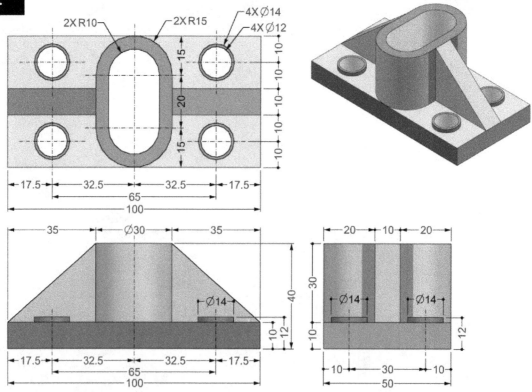

P-58

EX-113

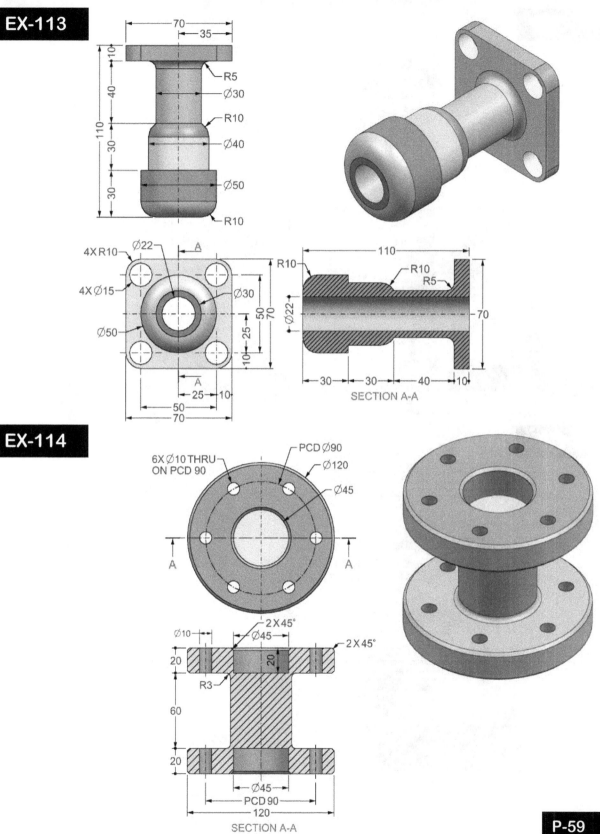

70
35
R5
Ø30
R10
Ø40
Ø50
R10
110
10
40
30
30

4X R10
Ø22
A
4X Ø15
Ø30
Ø50
50
70
25
10
A
25
10
50
70

R10
R10
R5
Ø22
110
70
30
30
40
10
SECTION A-A

EX-114

6X Ø10 THRU
ON PCD 90
PCD Ø90
Ø120
Ø45
A
A

Ø10
2 X 45°
Ø45
2 X 45°
20
20
R3
60
20
Ø45
PCD 90
120
SECTION A-A

EX-115

Ø120
6X Ø10
6X Ø8
PCD Ø90
Ø68
Ø45

A ⊢ ⊣ A

Ø120
Ø68
Ø10
R2
10
10
20
120
60
20
10
PCD 90

Ø120
PCD 90
Ø68
Ø45
Ø10
2 X 45°
40
20
20
R3
60
60
R3
Ø8
Ø55
Ø50
20
20
20
Ø45
Ø8

SECTION A-A

EX-116

120
100
10
25
50
25
10
4X Ø10
4X R5
25
A
30
50
25
15
10
Ø30
Ø20

20
80
50
R5
45
20
120

80
20
70
25
Ø10
30
R5
10
100
120

SECTION A-A

P-60

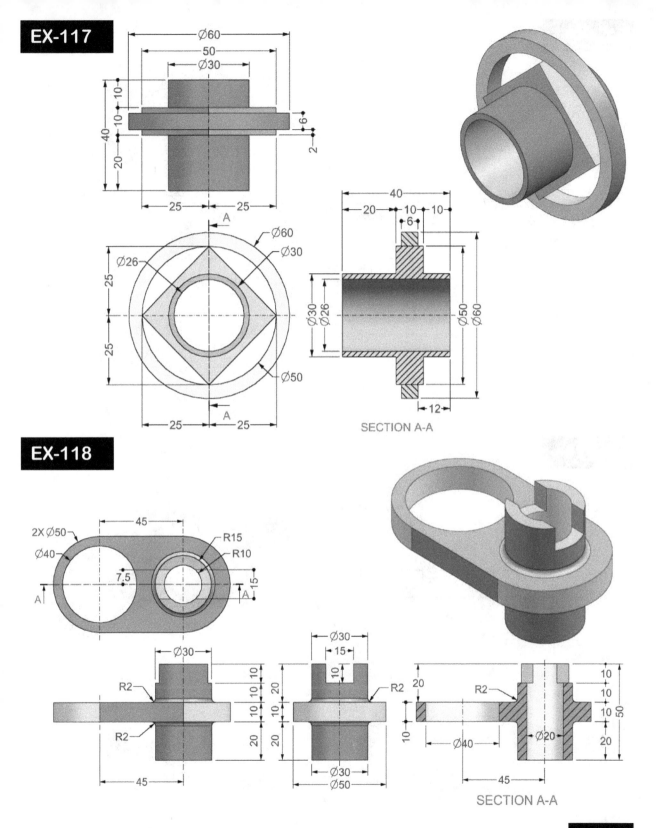

EX-117

Ø60
50
Ø30
40
10
10
20
6
2
25 25

A

Ø60
Ø30
Ø26
25
25
Ø50
25 25
A

40
20 10 10
6
Ø30
Ø26
Ø50
Ø60
12

SECTION A-A

EX-118

2X Ø50
Ø40
R15
R10
45
7.5
15
A A

R2
Ø30
10 10
10 10
20
R2
45

Ø30
15
10
20
10
20
R2
Ø30
Ø50

20
R2
10
Ø40
Ø20
45
10
10
10
20
50

SECTION A-A

P-61

EX-119

2X R20

Ø140
70
2X R25

25
50

Ø55
Ø75
Ø100
Ø180
Ø190

SECTION A-A

Ø190
Ø55

A

R25

25
50

A
Ø75
Ø190

Ø75
Ø55
Ø190
Ø180
Ø100

EX-120

Ø50
Ø60
10
15
20
20
20
40
20
15
45
100

R15
A
Ø50
Ø70
Ø70
Ø40
Ø20
Ø30
Ø60
100
100
A

Ø50
Ø30
Ø60
Ø40
10
90
15
20
20
20
20
15
Ø20
40
45
100
100

SECTION A-A

P-62

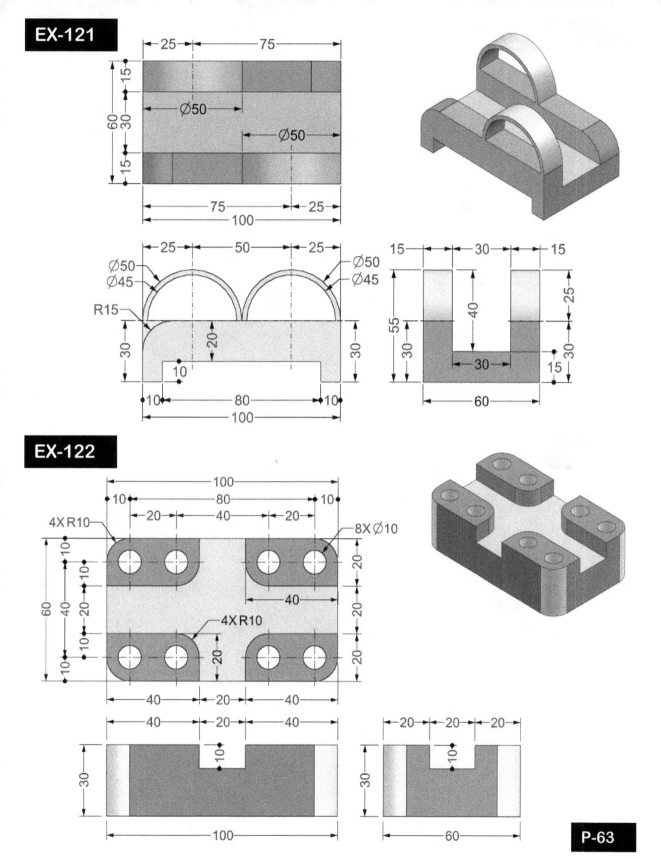

EX-121

EX-122

P-63

EX-123

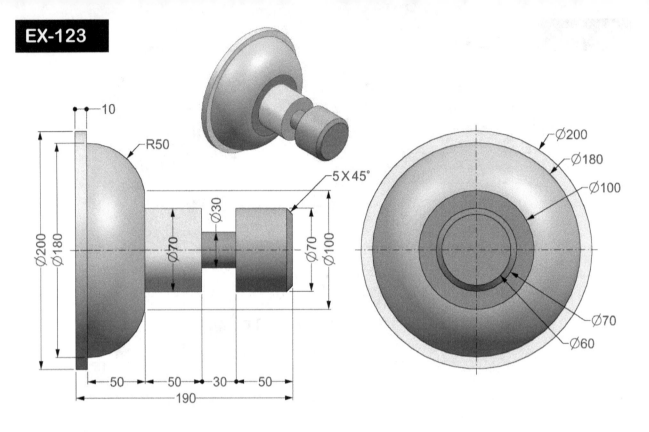

R50
10
Ø200
Ø180
Ø70
Ø30
5×45°
Ø70
Ø100
50
50
30
50
190

Ø200
Ø180
Ø100
Ø70
Ø60

EX-124

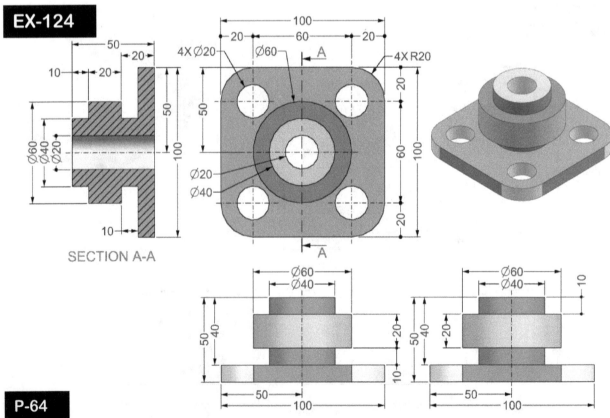

50
20
10
20
50
100
Ø60
Ø40
Ø20
10

SECTION A-A

100
20
60
20
4X Ø20
Ø60
A
4X R20
20
50
60
100
Ø20
Ø40
20
A

Ø60
Ø40
50
40
20
10

Ø60
Ø40
10
50
40
20

50
100

50
100

EX-125

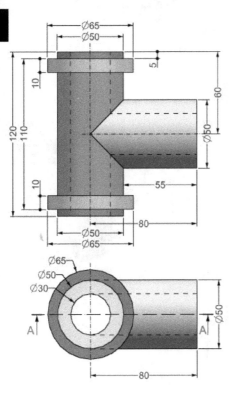

Ø65
Ø50
5
10
120
110
60
Ø50
10
55
Ø50
80
Ø65

Ø65
Ø50
Ø30
A
A
Ø50
80

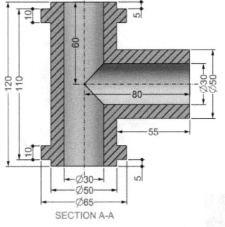

10
5
60
120
110
Ø30
Ø50
80
55
10
5
Ø30
Ø50
Ø65
SECTION A-A

EX-126

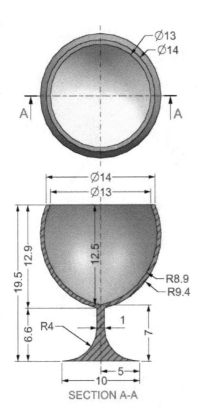

Ø13
Ø14
A
A

Ø14
Ø13
19.5
12.9
12.5
R8.9
R9.4
6.6
R4
1
7
5
10
SECTION A-A

P-65

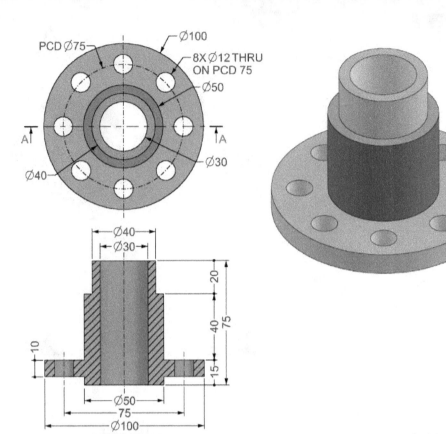

PCD Ø75
Ø100
8X Ø12 THRU
ON PCD 75
Ø50
Ø40
Ø30
A — A

Ø40
Ø30
20
75
40
10
15
Ø50
75
Ø100

SECTION A-A

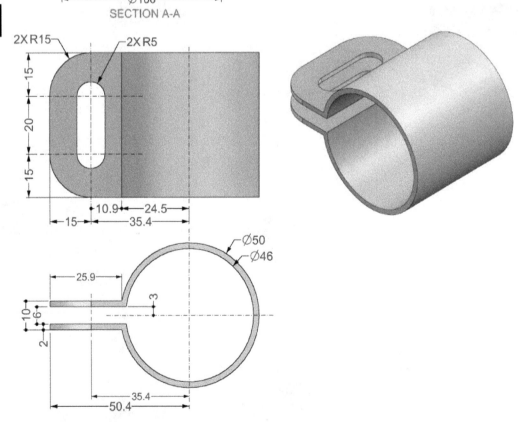

2X R15
2X R5
15
20
15
10.9
24.5
35.4
15

Ø50
Ø46
25.9
3
10
6
2
35.4
50.4

EX-129

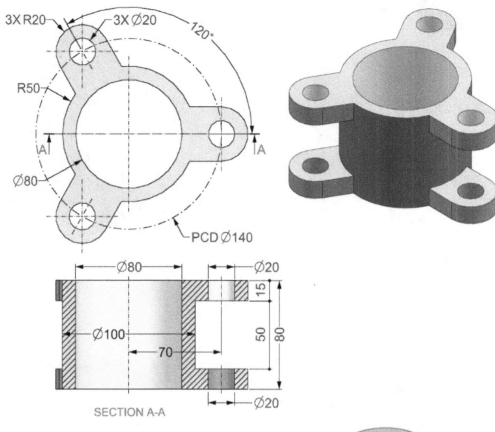

3X R20 3X Ø20 120°

R50

Ø80

PCD Ø140

Ø80 Ø20

15

Ø100

70

50 80

Ø20

SECTION A-A

EX-130

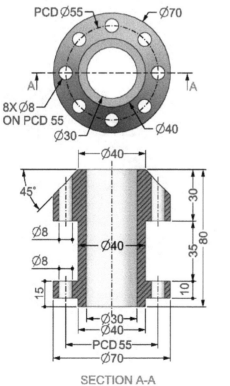

PCD Ø55 Ø70

8X Ø8
ON PCD 55

Ø30 Ø40

A A

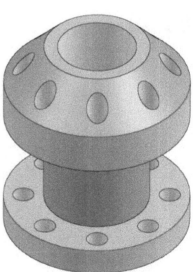

Ø40

45°

30

Ø8

Ø40

80

Ø8

35

15

10

Ø30
Ø40

PCD 55

Ø70

SECTION A-A

EX-131

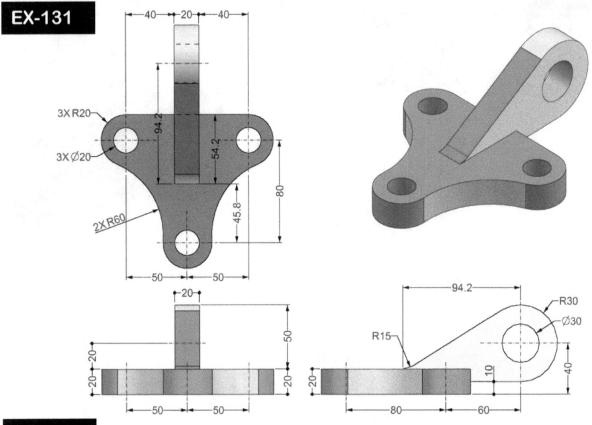

EX-132

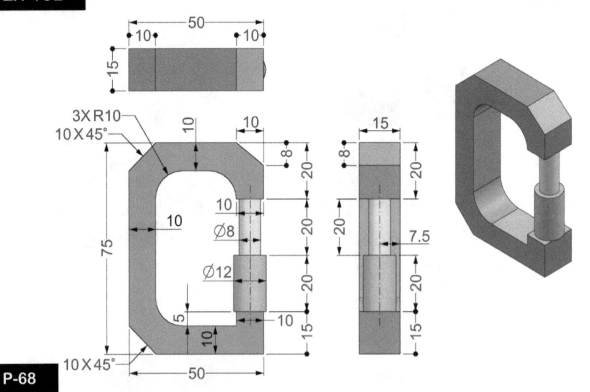

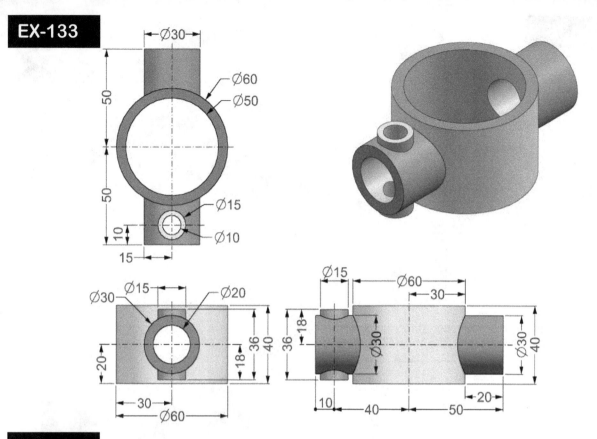

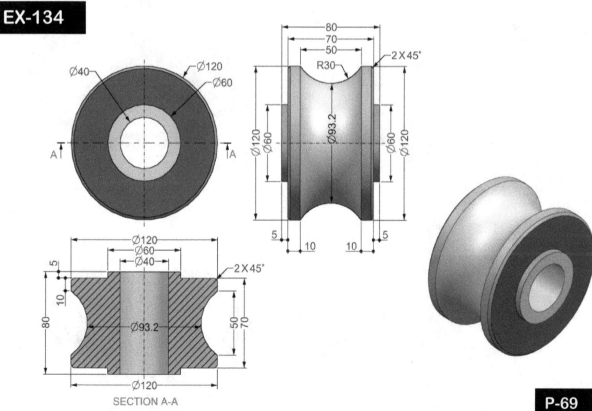

SECTION A-A

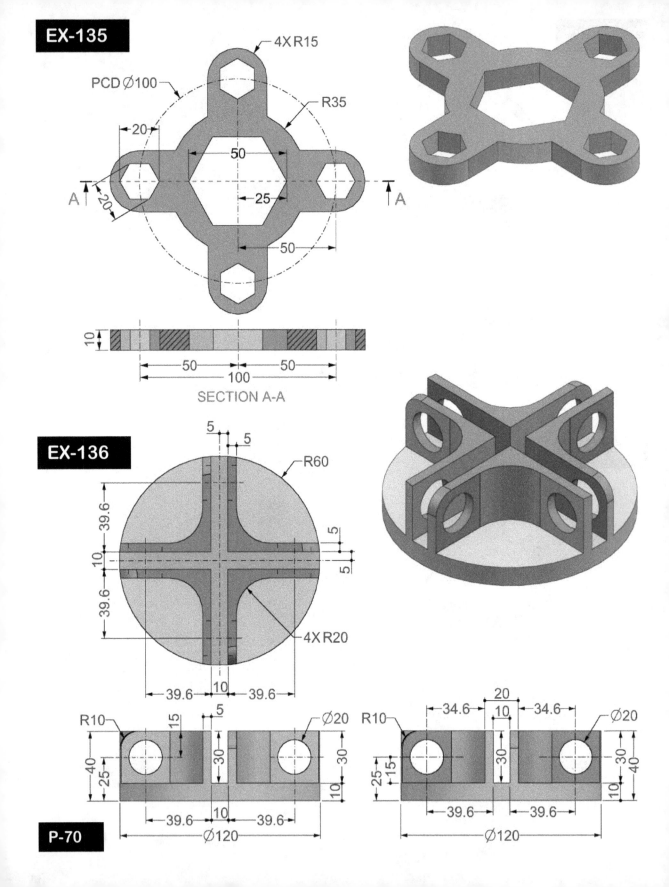

EX-135

4X R15

PCD Ø100

R35

20

50

25

20

A — A

50

10

50 — 50

100

SECTION A-A

EX-136

5

5

R60

39.6

5

10

5

39.6

4X R20

39.6 — 10 — 39.6

R10

15

5

Ø20

40

25

30

30

10

39.6 — 10 — 39.6

Ø120

R10

20

34.6 — 10 — 34.6

Ø20

25

15

30

30

10

40

39.6 — 39.6

Ø120

P-70

EX-137

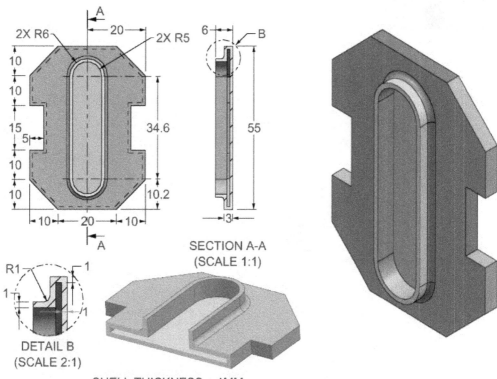

2X R6
20
2X R5
10
10
15
5
10
10
10
20
10
34.6
10.2
A
A

6
B
55
3

SECTION A-A
(SCALE 1:1)

R1
1
1
1

DETAIL B
(SCALE 2:1)

SHELL THICKNESS = 1MM
ALL INSIDE WALL THICKNESS

EX-138

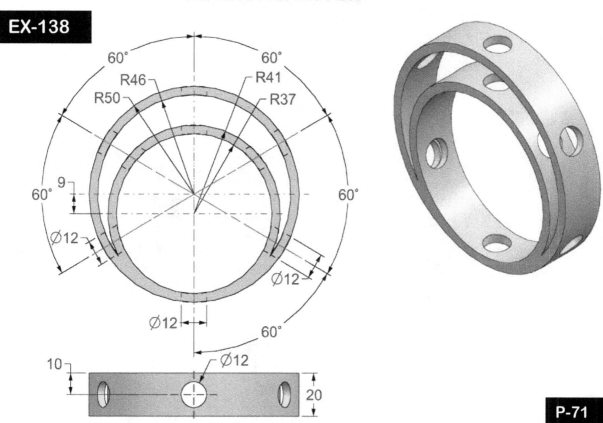

60°
60°
R46
R41
R50
R37
60°
9
60°
Ø12
Ø12
Ø12
60°
Ø12

10
Ø12
20

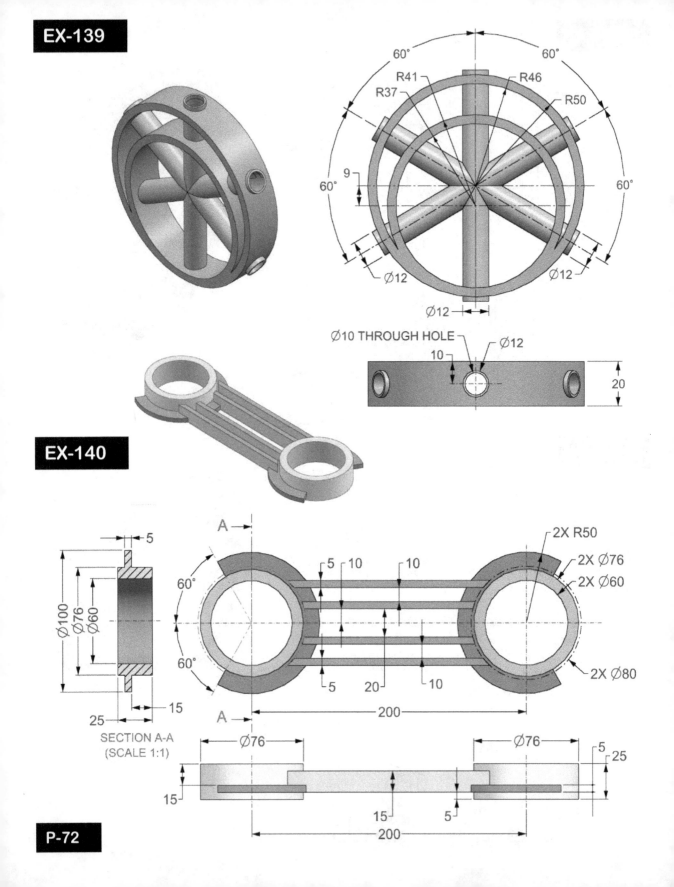

EX-139

60° 60°
R41 R46
R37 R50
60° 60°
9
60° 60°
∅12 ∅12
∅12

∅10 THROUGH HOLE ∅12
10
20

EX-140

A

5
2X R50
2X ∅76
60° 5 10 10 2X ∅60
∅100
∅76
∅60
60° 5 20 10 2X ∅80
15 A 200
25
SECTION A-A ∅76 ∅76
(SCALE 1:1) 5
25
15 15 5
200

P-72

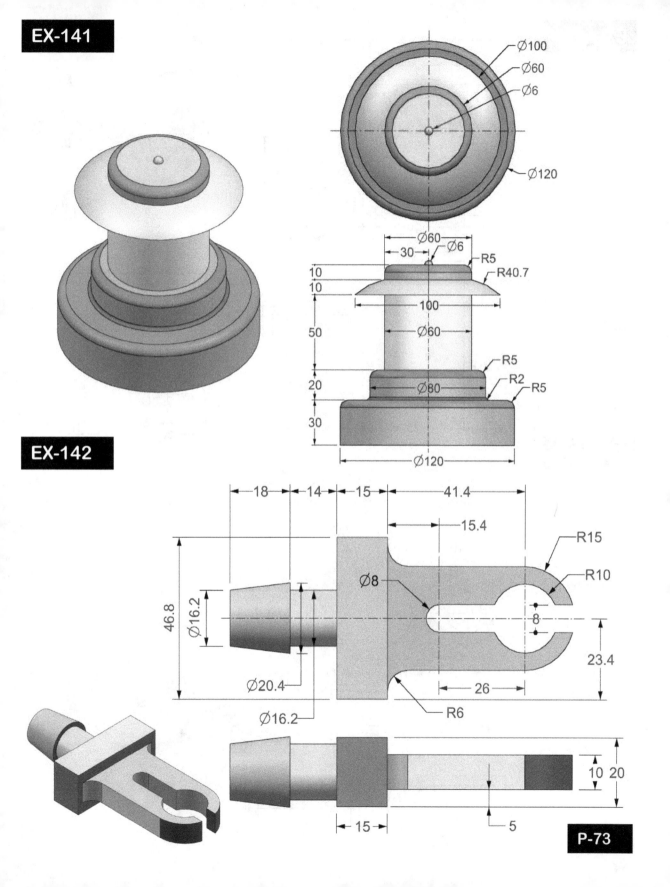

EX-141

Ø100
Ø60
Ø6
Ø120

Ø60
30
Ø6
R5
R40.7
10
10
100
50
Ø60
R5
20
Ø80
R2 R5
30
Ø120

EX-142

18   14   15   41.4
15.4
R15
R10
Ø8
46.8
Ø16.2
8
Ø20.4
23.4
26
Ø16.2
R6

10 20
15
5

P-73

EX-143

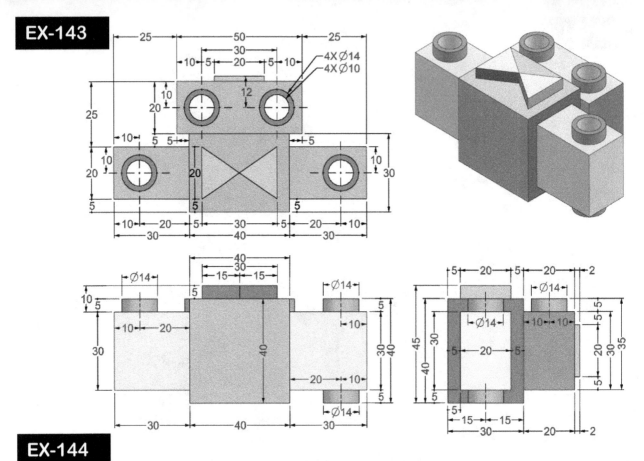

EX-144

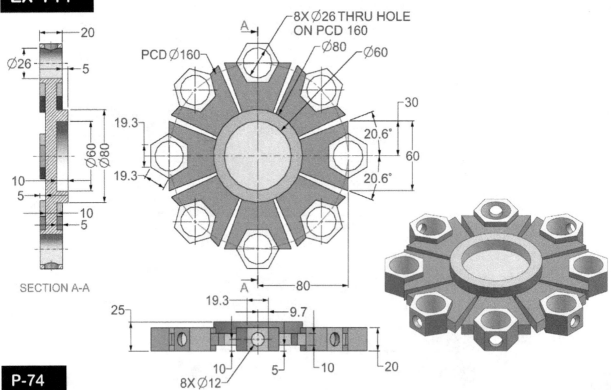

8X Ø26 THRU HOLE ON PCD 160

PCD Ø160

Ø80

Ø60

SECTION A-A

8X Ø12

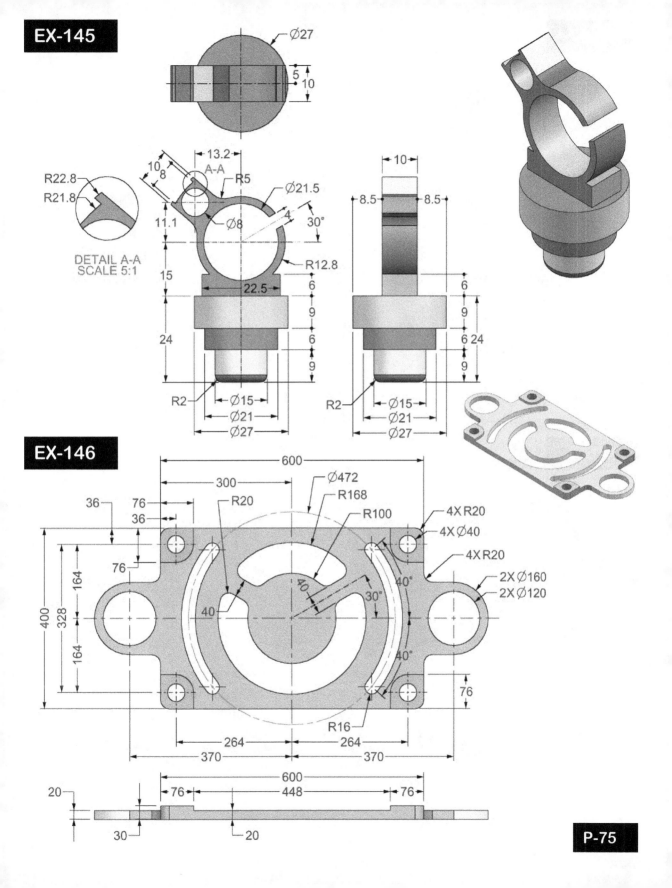

EX-145

Ø27
5
10

R22.8
R21.8
DETAIL A-A
SCALE 5:1

13.2
10
8
A-A
R5
Ø21.5
Ø8
11.1
4
30°
R12.8
15
22.5
6
9
24
6
9
R2
Ø15
Ø21
Ø27

10
8.5
8.5
6
9
6 24
9
R2
Ø15
Ø21
Ø27

EX-146

600
300
Ø472
R168
R100
36
76
R20
4X R20
36
4X Ø40
76
4X R20
164
2X Ø160
400
328
40
2X Ø120
164
40
30°
40°
40°
76
R16
264
264
76
370
370

600
20
76
448
76
30
20

Ø40
Ø20
120°
120°
10
60

R10
Ø40
200
79.6
Ø20
15
60
R15

2X Ø100
2X Ø80
Ø50
R45
R40
Ø30
51.6
100
100
A
A

Ø90
Ø50
10
40
15
10
100
100

Ø90
Ø80
Ø50
Ø30
Ø80
Ø80
15
10
10
40
15
100
100

SECTION A-A

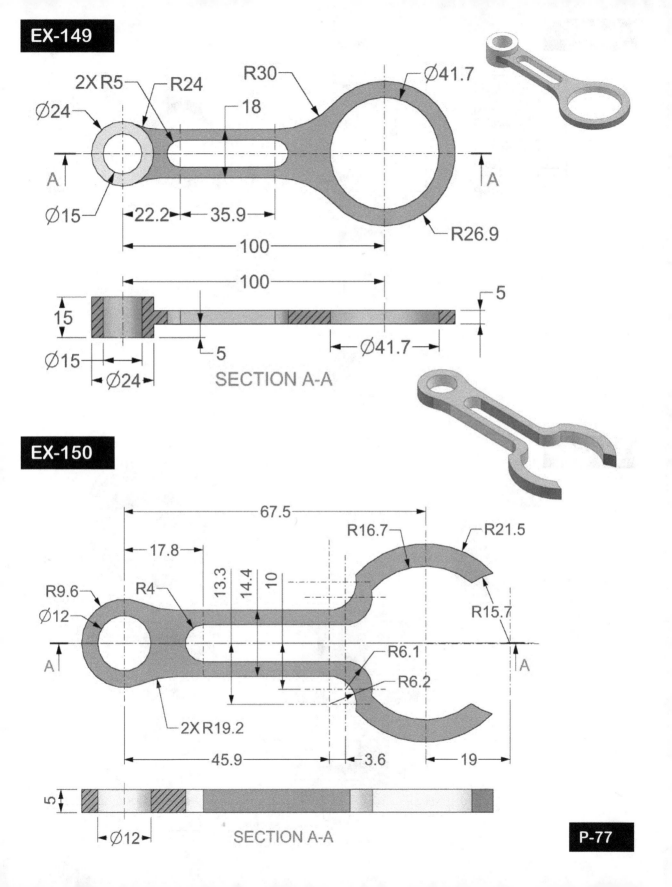

EX-149

2X R5   R24   R30   ∅41.7
∅24   18
R26.9
∅15   2X R5
22.2   35.9
100

100
15   5
∅15   5   ∅41.7
∅24   SECTION A-A

EX-150

67.5
17.8   R16.7   R21.5
13.3   14.4   10
R9.6   R4   R15.7
∅12
A   R6.1   A
R6.2
2X R19.2
45.9   3.6   19

5
∅12   SECTION A-A

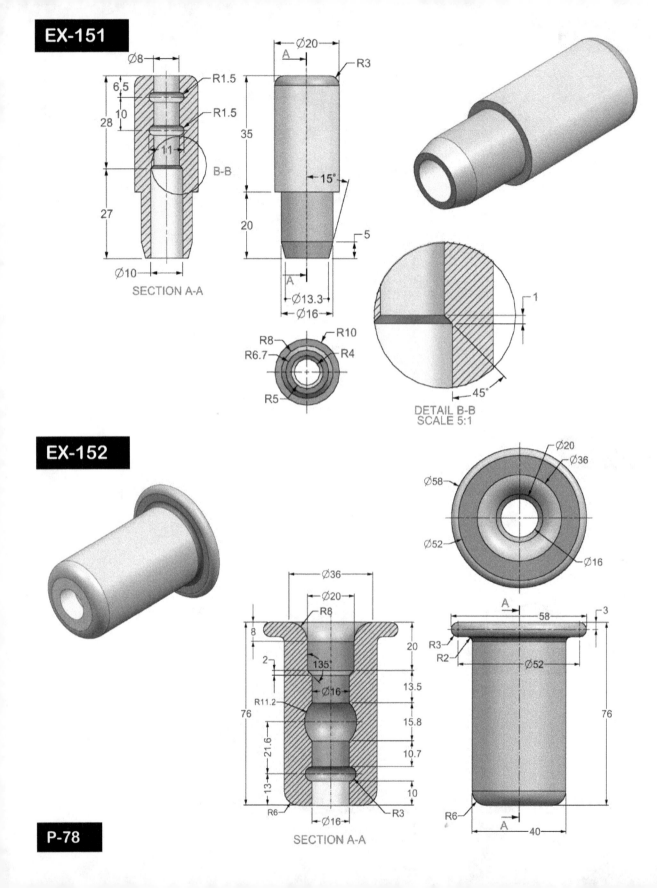

EX-151

Ø8
6,5
10
28
1:1
R1.5
R1.5
B-B
27
Ø10
SECTION A-A

Ø20
A
R3
35
15°
20
5
A
Ø13.3
Ø16

R8
R6.7
R10
R4
R5

1
45°
DETAIL B-B
SCALE 5:1

EX-152

Ø20
Ø36
Ø58
Ø52
Ø16

Ø36
Ø20
R8
8
2
135°
Ø16
76
R11.2
21.6
13
R6
Ø16
R3
20
13.5
15.8
10.7
10
SECTION A-A

A
58
3
R3
R2
Ø52
76
R6
A
40

P-78

EX-153

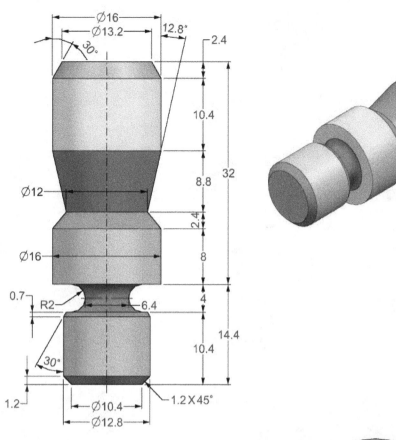

Ø16
Ø13.2
12.8°
2.4
30°
10.4
32
8.8
Ø12
2.4
Ø16
8
0.7
R2
6.4
4
14.4
10.4
30°
1.2
Ø10.4
Ø12.8
1.2 X 45°

EX-154

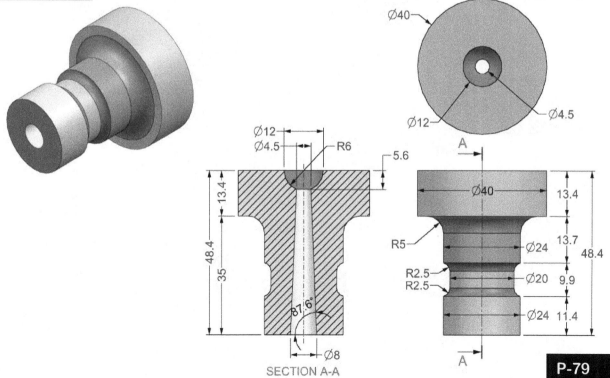

Ø40
Ø12
Ø4.5

Ø12
Ø4.5
R6
5.6
13.4
48.4
35
A
Ø40
13.4
R5
13.7
Ø24
R2.5
R2.5
Ø20
9.9
Ø24
11.4
48.4
87.6°
Ø8
SECTION A-A
A

P-79

EX-155

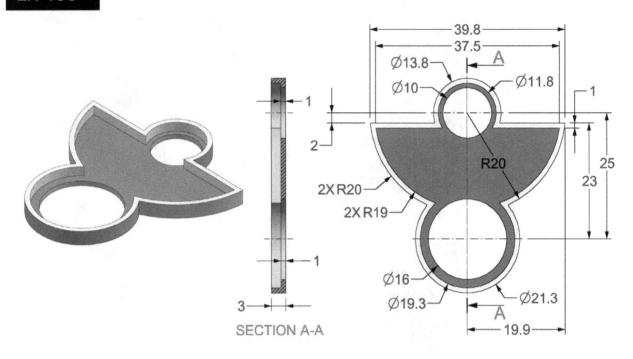

SECTION A-A

EX-156

SECTION A-A

P-80

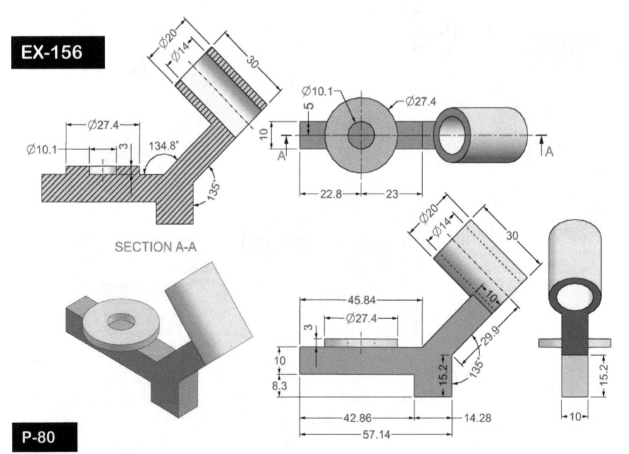

EX-157

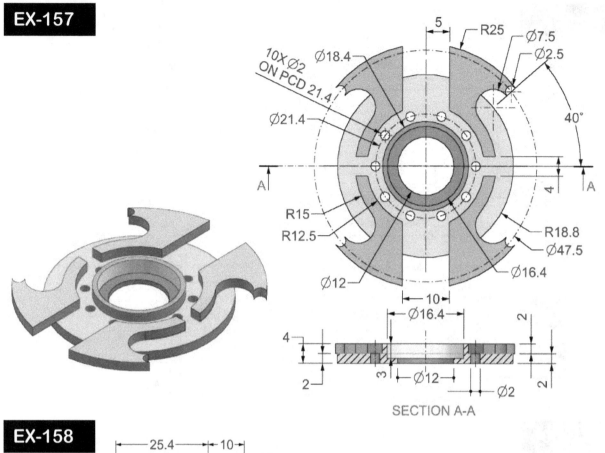

10X Ø2 ON PCD 21.4
Ø18.4
5
R25
Ø7.5
Ø2.5
40°
Ø21.4
4
R15
R12.5
R18.8
Ø47.5
Ø12
Ø16.4
10

SECTION A-A

Ø16.4
4
2
3
Ø12
Ø2
2
2

EX-158

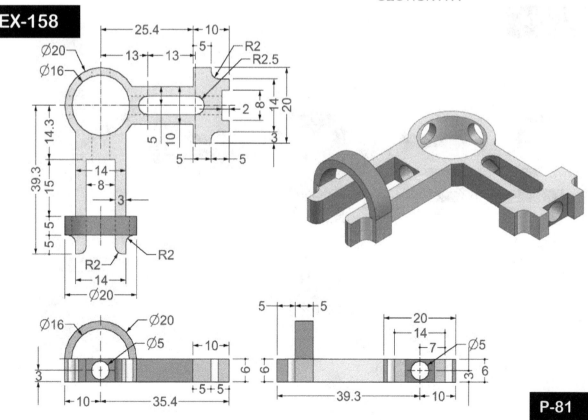

Ø20
Ø16
25.4
10
13
13
5
R2
R2.5
2
8
14
20
10
5
5
5
14.3
39.3
15
14
8
3
5 5
R2
R2
14
Ø20

Ø16
Ø20
Ø5
10
3
10
35.4
5 5

5
5
20
14
7
Ø5
6
6
3
6
39.3
10

EX-159

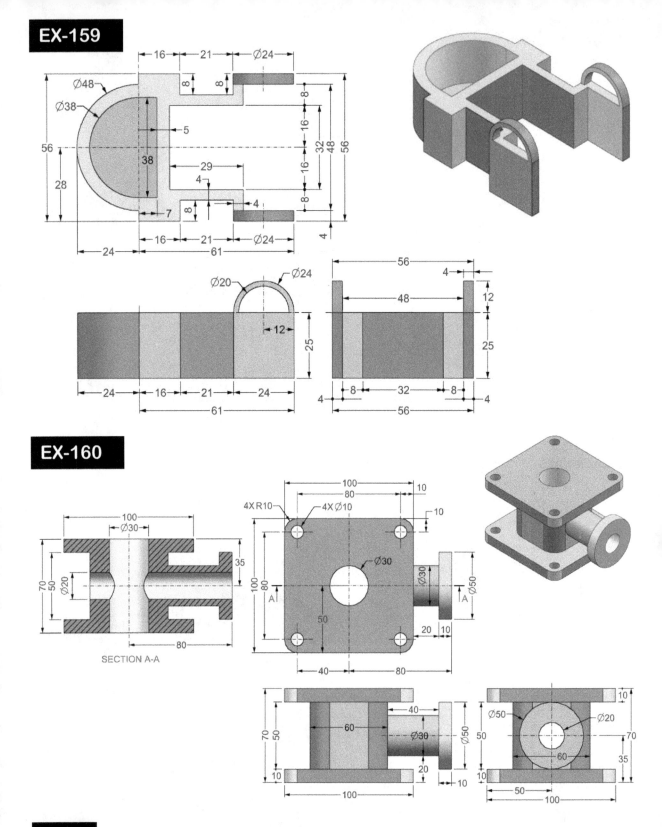

EX-160

SECTION A-A

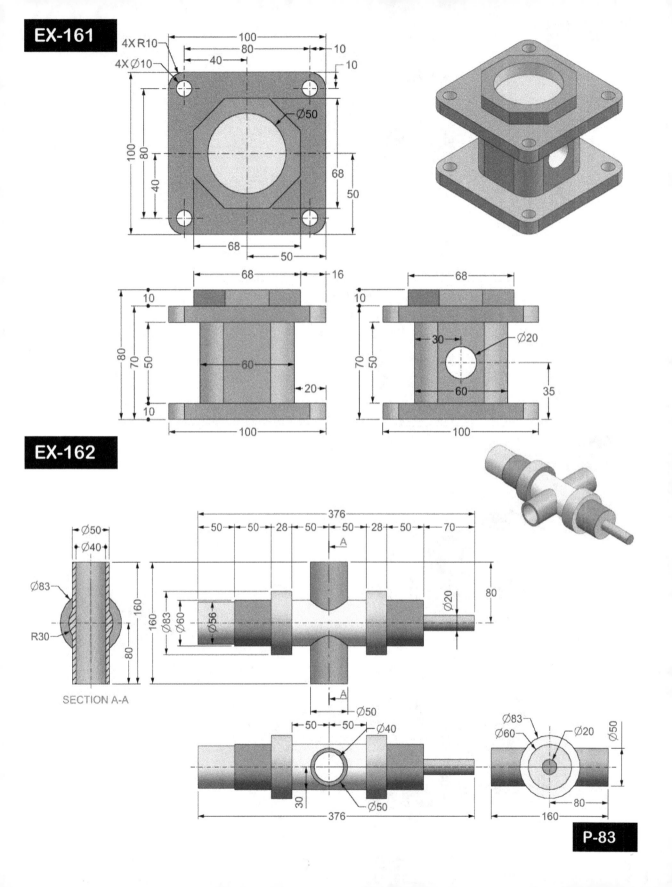

EX-161

4X R10
4X Ø10
100
80
40
10
10
Ø50
100
80
40
68
50
68
50

68
16
10
80
70
50
60
20
10
100

68
10
70
50
30
Ø20
60
35
100

EX-162

376
50 50 28 50 50 28 50 70
A

Ø50
Ø40
Ø83
R30
160
160
80
Ø83
Ø60
Ø56
Ø20
80

SECTION A-A
A
Ø50

50 50 Ø40
Ø50
30
Ø50
376

Ø83
Ø60
Ø20
Ø50
80
160

P-83

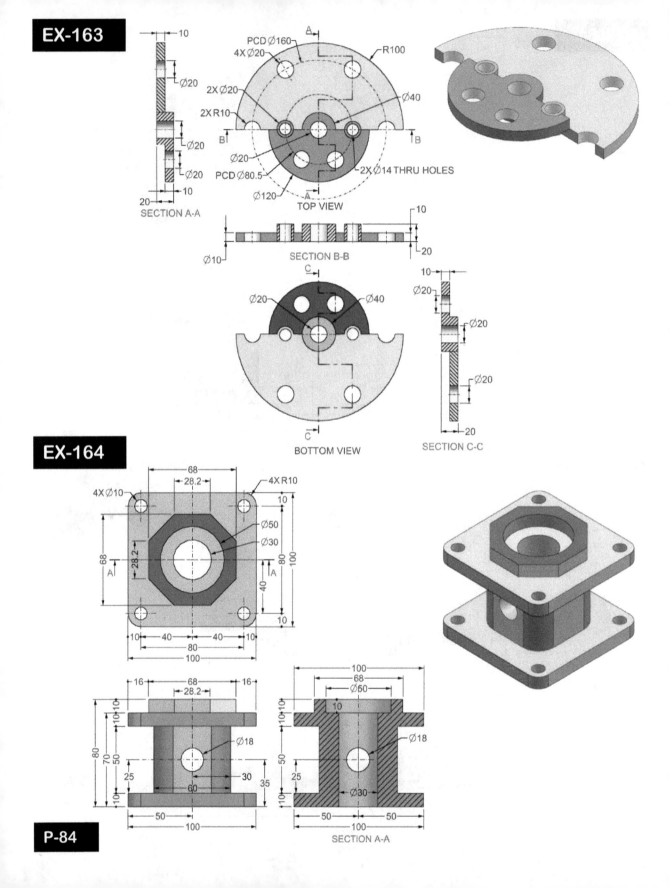

EX-163

PCD Ø160
4X Ø20
2X Ø20
2X R10
R100
Ø40
Ø20
2X Ø14 THRU HOLES
PCD Ø80.5
Ø120
10
Ø20
Ø20
Ø20
10
20

SECTION A-A

TOP VIEW

10
20
Ø10

SECTION B-B

Ø20
Ø40

C

C

BOTTOM VIEW

10
Ø20
Ø20
Ø20
20

SECTION C-C

EX-164

68
28.2
4X R10
4X Ø10
10
Ø50
Ø30
68
28.2
80
100
A
A
40
10
10
40
40
10
80
100

16
68
16
28.2
10 10
Ø18
80
70
50
25
30
10
50
100
35
60

100
68
Ø50
10 10
10
50
Ø18
25
50
50
100
Ø30

SECTION A-A

P-84

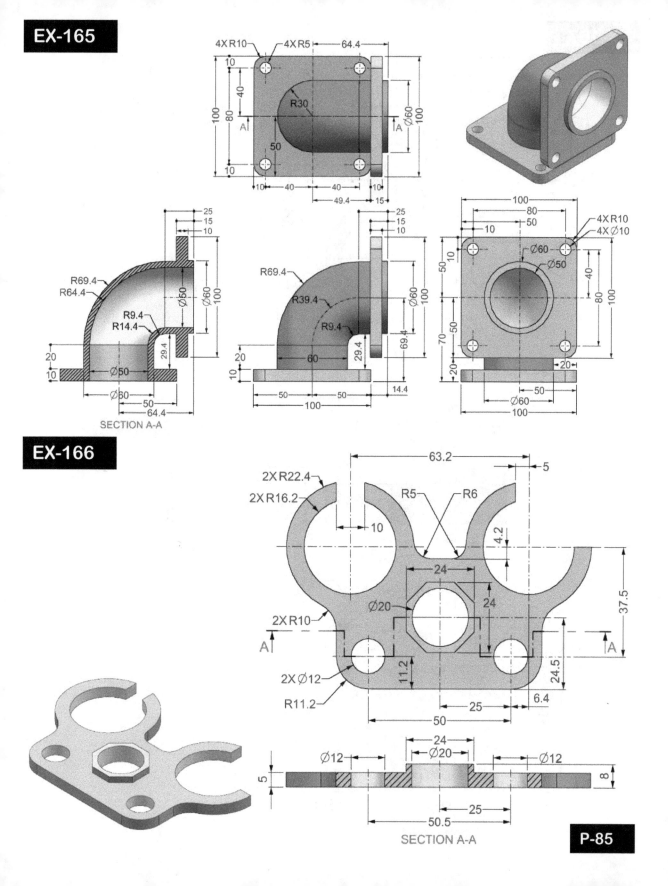

EX-165

4X R10   4X R5   64.4
10
40
80
100
R30
A
50
10
A
10   40   40   10
49.4   15
Ø60
100

25
15
10
R69.4
R64.4
R9.4
R14.4
Ø50
Ø60
100
29.4
20
10
Ø50
Ø60
50
64.4
SECTION A-A

25
15
10
R69.4
R39.4
R9.4
Ø60
100
69.4
20
10
60
29.4
50   50
100
14.4

100
80
50
10
4X R10
4X Ø10
Ø60
Ø50
50   10
50
70
40
80
100
20
50
Ø60
100
20

EX-166

63.2   5
2X R22.4
2X R16.2
R5   R6
10
4.2
24
Ø20
24
37.5
2X R10
A   A
11.2
24.5
2X Ø12
6.4
R11.2
25
50

24
Ø12   Ø20   Ø12
5
8
25
50.5
SECTION A-A

P-85

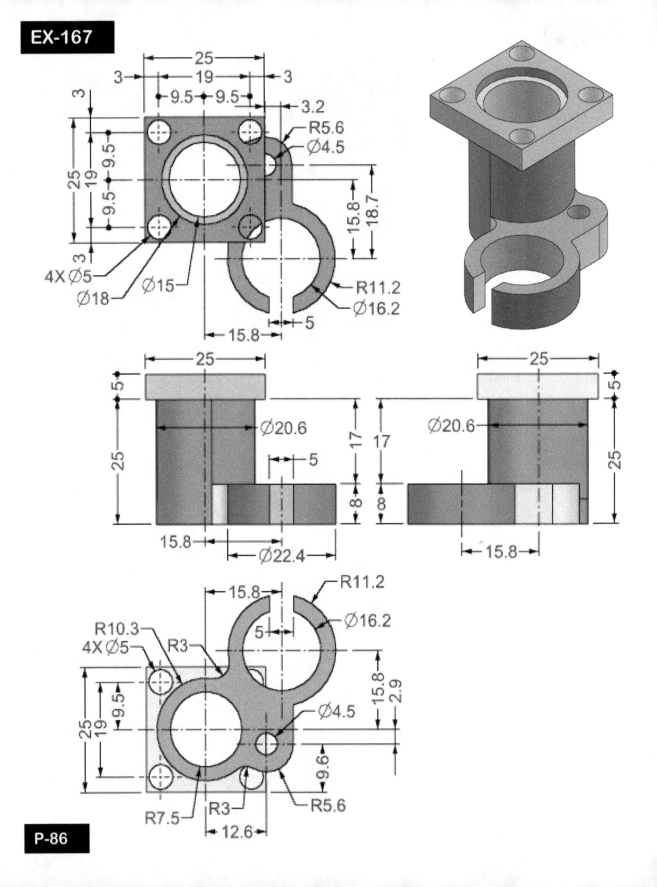

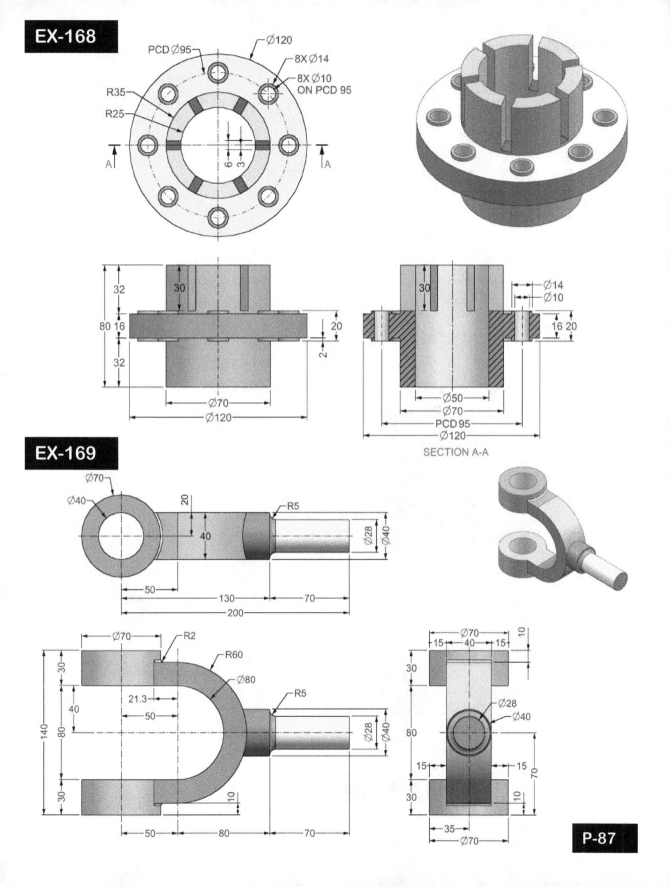

EX-168

PCD Ø95
Ø120
8X Ø14
8X Ø10
ON PCD 95
R35
R25
6
3
A
A

32
30
80 16
32
20
2
Ø70
Ø120

30
Ø14
Ø10
16 20
Ø50
Ø70
PCD 95
Ø120
SECTION A-A

EX-169

Ø70
Ø40
20
R5
40
Ø28
Ø40
50
130
70
200

Ø70
R2
R60
Ø80
R5
30
21.3
40
50
80
140
Ø28
Ø40
30
10
50
80
70

Ø70
15
40
15
10
30
Ø28
Ø40
80
70
15
15
30
10
35
Ø70

P-87

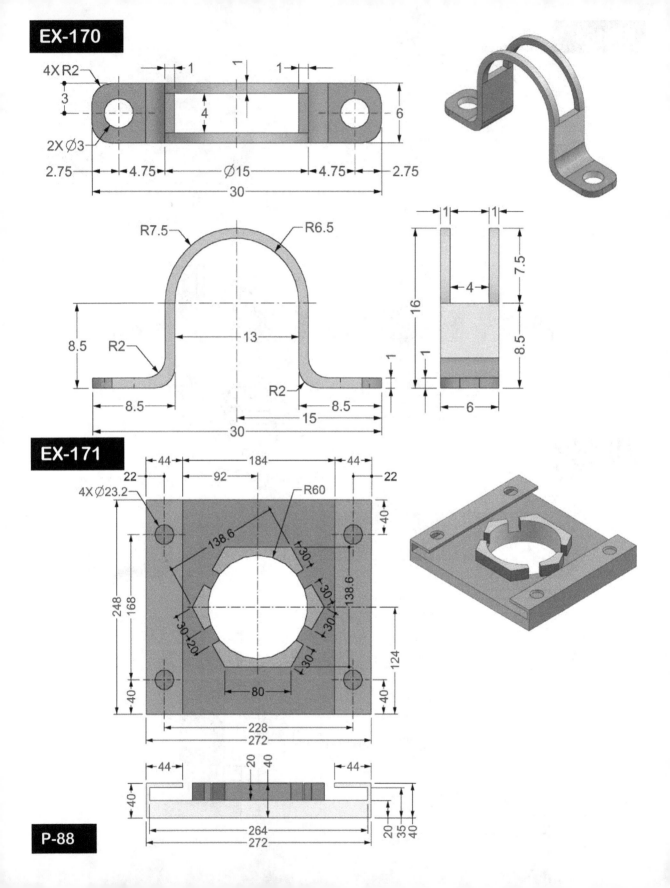

EX-170

4X R2
3
2X Ø3
2.75 — 4.75 — Ø15 — 4.75 — 2.75
30
1   1   1
4
6

R7.5   R6.5
R2
8.5   13   R2
8.5   8.5
15
30

1 1
7.5
4
16
8.5
1
1
6

EX-171

44 — 184 — 44
22   92   22
4X Ø23.2
R60
40
138.6
30
30
248   168   138.6
30   30
30   20   30
124
30
80
40
228
272

44   20 40   44
40
264   20 35 40
272

P-88

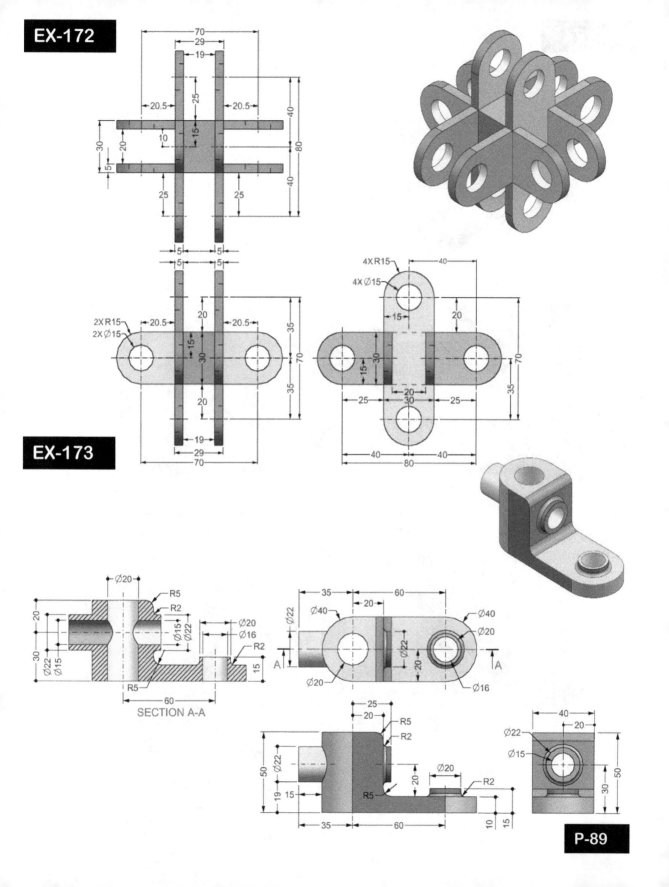

EX-172

EX-173

SECTION A-A

P-89

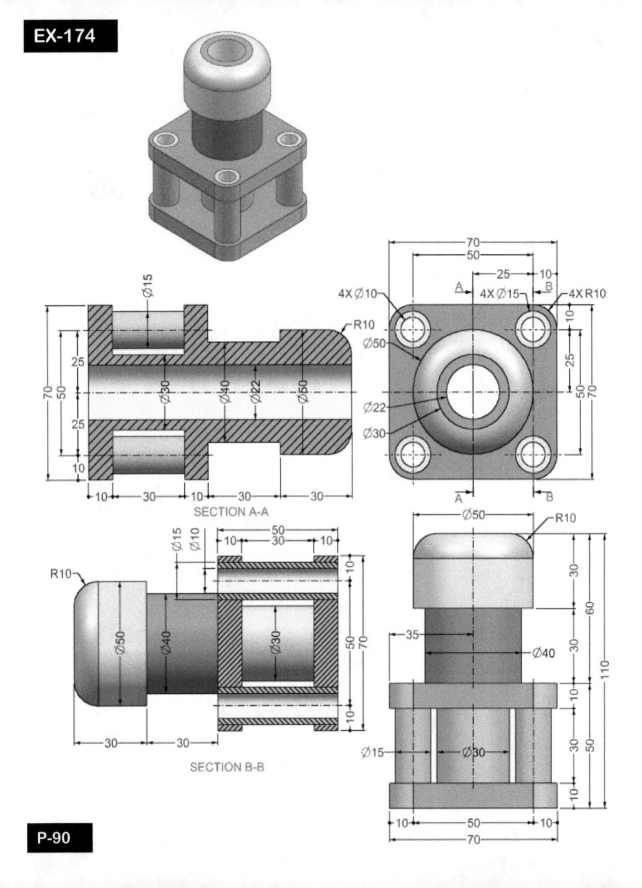

EX-174

P-90

Ø15

SECTION A-A

70
50
25
25
10
10 · 30 · 10 · 30 · 30

Ø30 Ø40 Ø22 Ø50
R10

70
50
25
10
4X Ø10
Ø50
Ø22
Ø30
A
A
B
B
4X Ø15
4X R10
10
25
50
70

Ø15
Ø10
50
10 · 30 · 10
R10
Ø50
Ø40
Ø30
30 · 30
10
50
70
10
SECTION B-B

Ø50
R10
30
60
110
35
Ø40
10
30
50
10
Ø15
Ø30
10 · 50 · 10
70

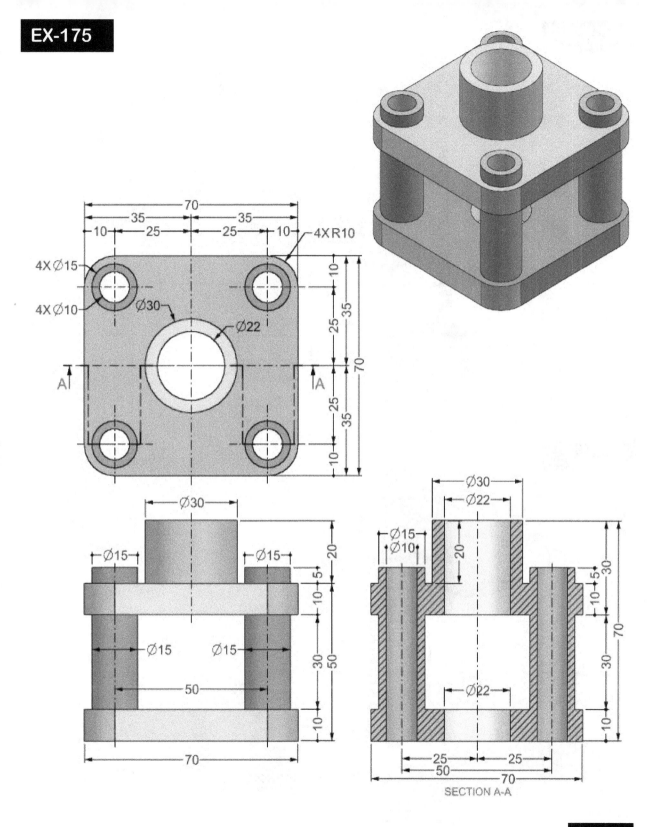

4X Ø15
4X Ø10
Ø30
Ø22
4X R10
70
35
35
10
25
25
10
10
25
35
70
35
25
10
A
A

Ø30
Ø15
Ø15
Ø15
Ø15
50
70
20
5
10
30
50
10

Ø30
Ø22
Ø15
Ø10
20
30
5
10
70
30
10
Ø22
25
25
50
70

SECTION A-A

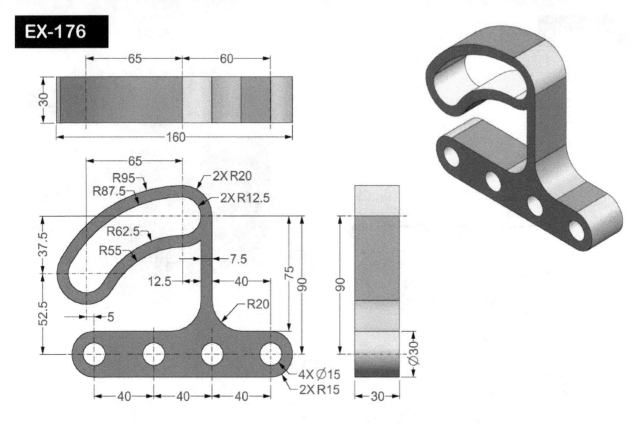

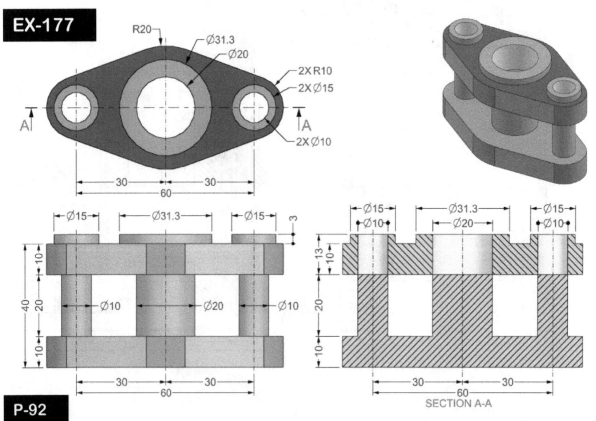

SECTION A-A

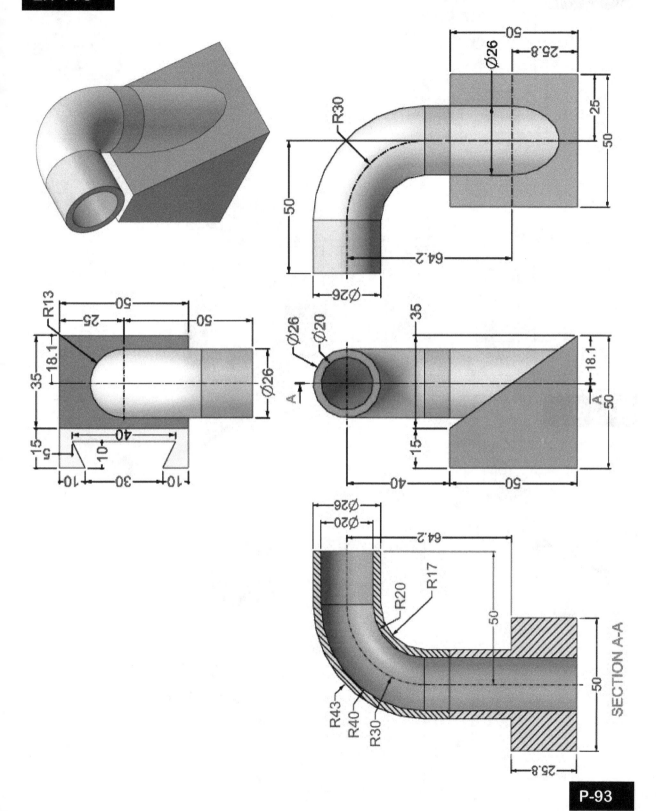

SECTION A-A

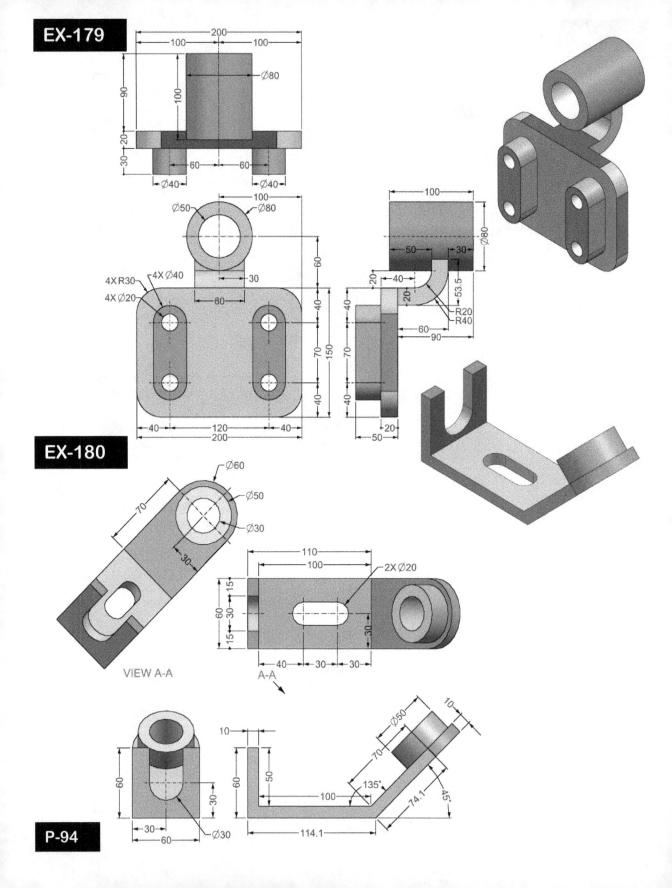

EX-179

EX-180

VIEW A-A

A-A

P-94

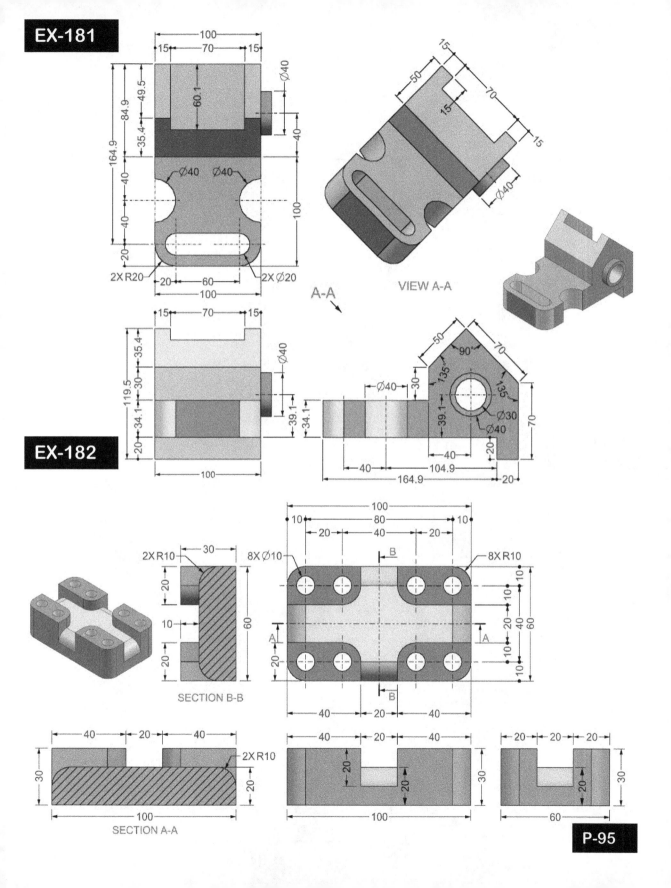

EX-181

EX-182

VIEW A-A

A-A

SECTION B-B

SECTION A-A

2X R10

8X Ø10

8X R10

2X R10

P-95

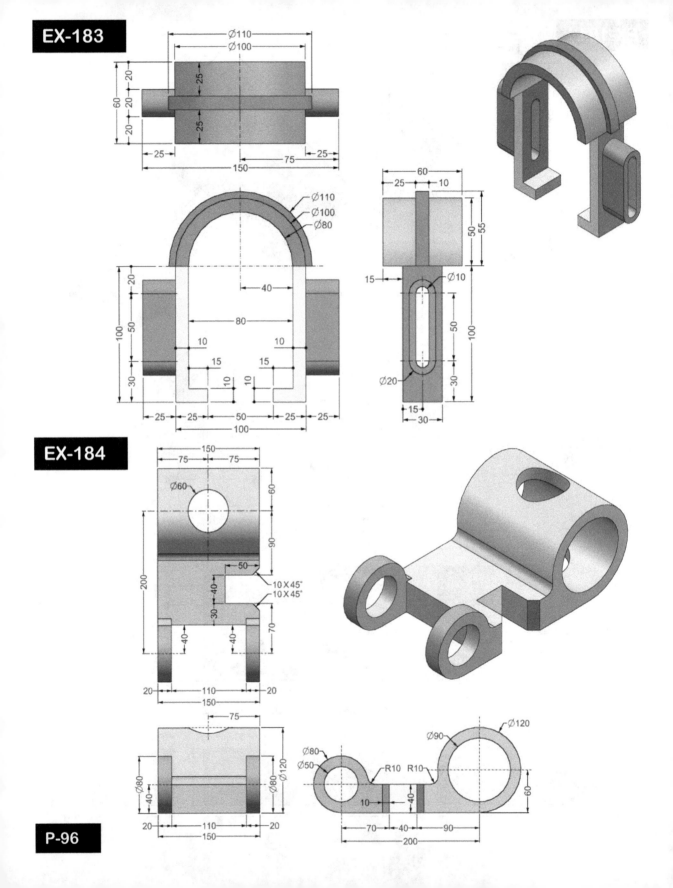

EX-183

Ø110
Ø100
20
20
60
20
25
25
25
75
25
150

Ø110
Ø100
Ø80
20
50
100
30
40
80
10
10
15
15
10
10
25
25
50
25
25
100

60
25
10
50
55
15
Ø10
50
100
30
Ø20
15
30

EX-184

150
75
75
Ø60
60
90
200
50
40
10 X 45°
30
10 X 45°
40
40
70
20
110
20
150

75
Ø80
Ø120
40
Ø80
20
110
20
150

Ø80
Ø50
Ø90
Ø120
R10 R10
60
10
40
70
40
90
200

P-96

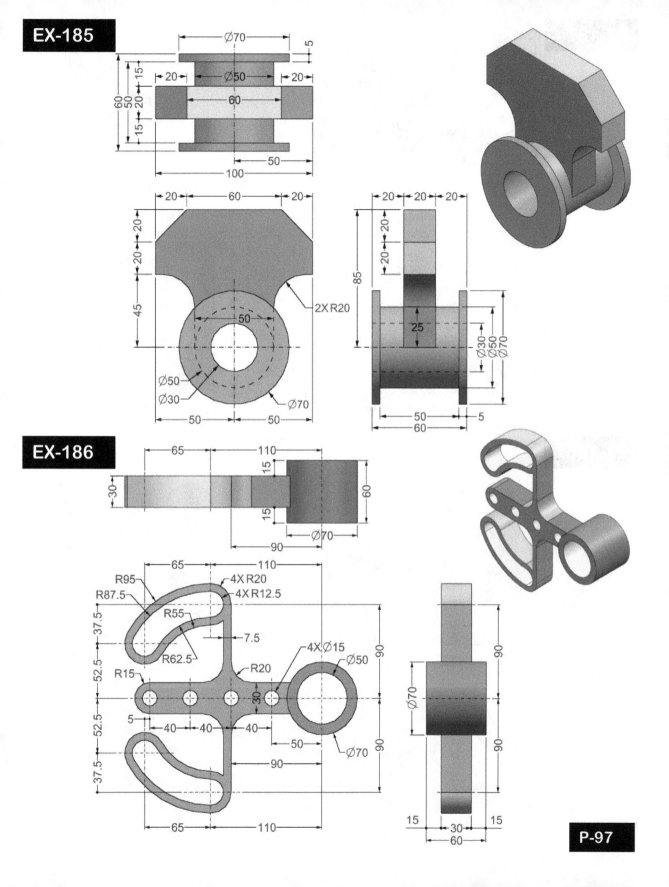

EX-185

Ø70
5
15
20 Ø50 20
60 50 60
20
15
50
100

20 60 20
20
20
45
50
Ø50
Ø30
50 50
Ø70
2X R20

20 20 20
20
20
85
25
Ø30
Ø50
Ø70
50
60
5

EX-186

65 110
30
15
15
Ø70
60
90

65 110
R95 4X R20
R87.5 4X R12.5
37.5 R55
R62.5 7.5
52.5 4X Ø15
R15 R20 Ø50
5 30
40 40 40
50
90
Ø70
52.5
37.5
65 110
90
90

90
Ø70
90
15 30 15
60

P-97

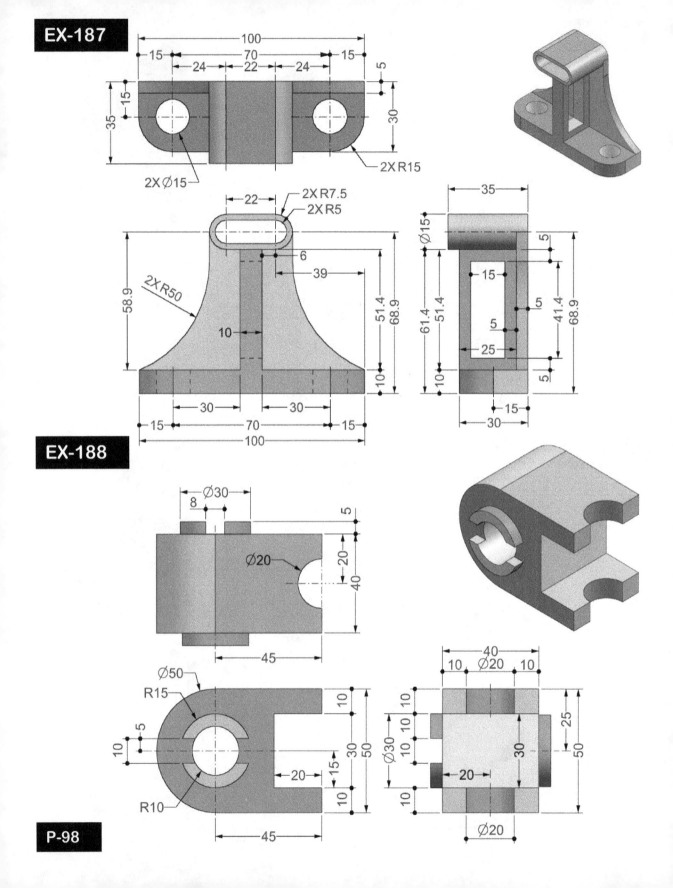

EX-187

100
15 — 70 — 15
24 — 22 — 24
5
35
15
30
2X Ø15
2X R15

22
2X R7.5
2X R5
6
39
58.9
2X R50
51.4
68.9
10
10
30 — 30
15 — 70 — 15
100

35
Ø15
5
15
61.4
51.4
68.9
5
41.4
5
25
10
15
30

EX-188

Ø30
8
5
Ø20
20
40
45

Ø50
R15
5
R10
10
10
30
50
20
15
10
45

40
10 — Ø20 — 10
10
Ø30
10
10
25
30
50
20
10
Ø20

P-98

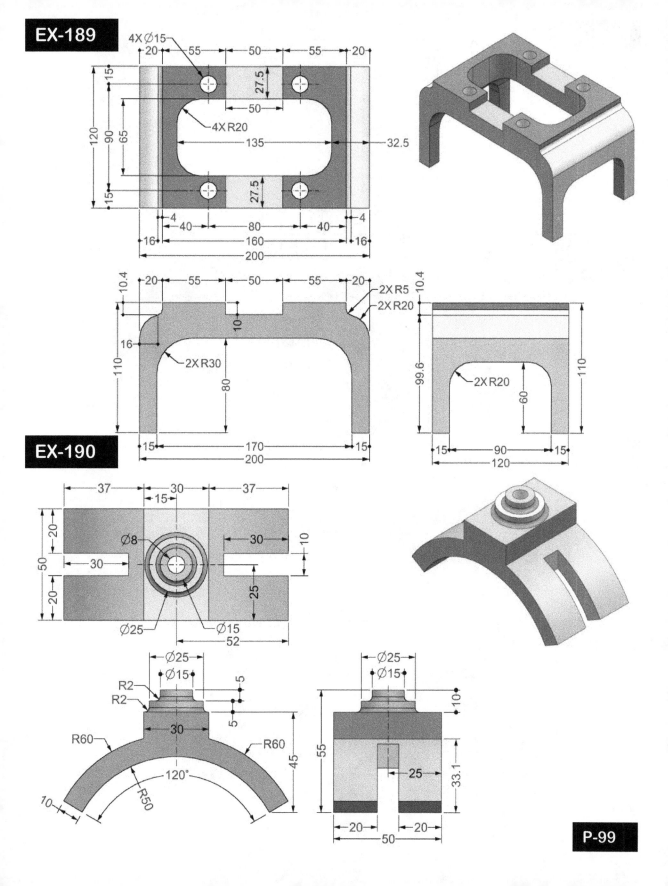

EX-189

4X Ø15
20 — 55 — 50 — 55 — 20
15
27.5
50
90
65
4X R20
135
32.5
15
27.5
4
40 — 80 — 40
4
16
160
16
200
120

10.4
20 — 55 — 50 — 55 — 20
2X R5
2X R20
10
16
110
2X R30
80
15 — 170 — 15
200

10.4
99.6
2X R20
60
110
15 — 90 — 15
120

EX-190

37 — 30 — 37
15
20
30
10
50
Ø8
30
25
Ø25
Ø15
52

Ø25
Ø15
R2
5
R2
10
30
R60
55
R60
45
120°
33.1
R50
25
10
20 — 20
50

P-99

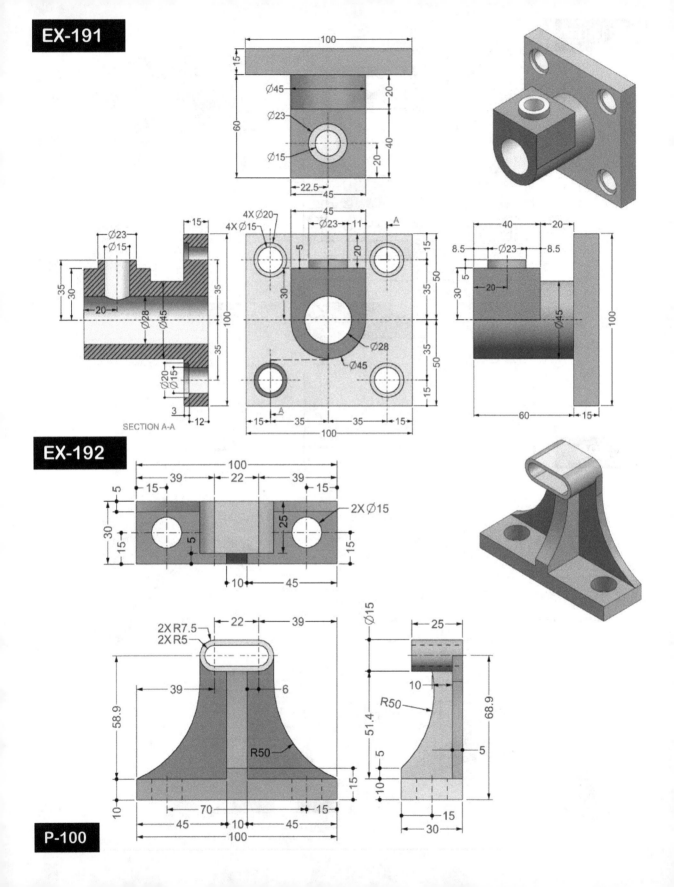

EX-191

EX-192

P-100

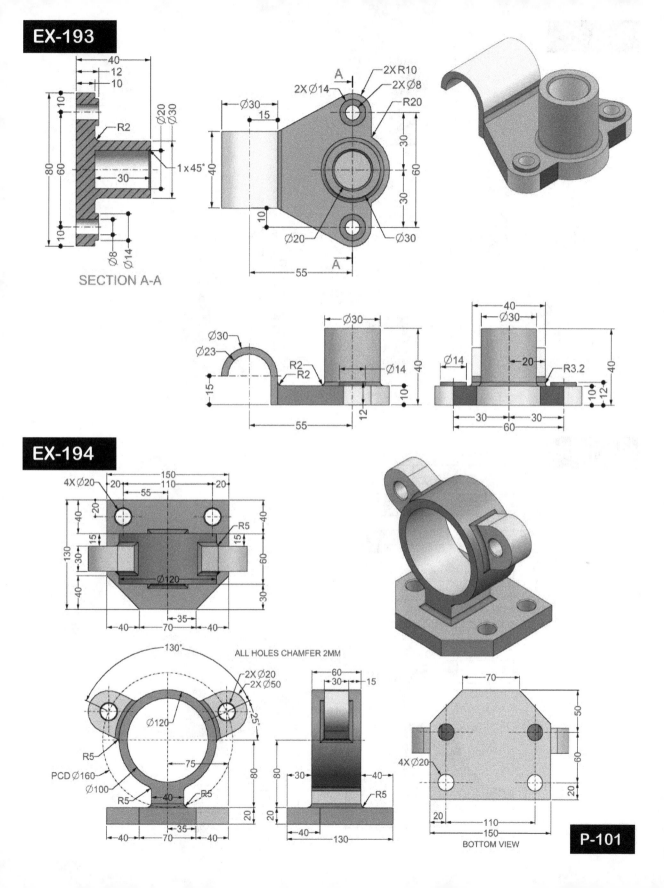

EX-193

SECTION A-A

40
12
10
10
Ø20
Ø30
R2
80
60
1 x 45°
30
10
Ø8
Ø14

2X Ø14
2X R10
2X Ø8
R20
A
Ø30
15
40
30
60
30
10
Ø20
Ø30
55
A

Ø30
Ø23
R2
R2
Ø14
40
15
10
12
55

40
Ø30
Ø14
20
R3.2
40
10
12
30
30
60

EX-194

4X Ø20
150
110
20
20
55
20
40
R5
15
15
130
30
60
40
Ø120
30
40
70
40
35

130°
ALL HOLES CHAMFER 2MM
2X Ø20
2X Ø50
25°
Ø120
R5
Ø100
75
PCD Ø160
R5
R5
80
40
40
70
40
35

60
30
15
80
30
40
20
R5
40
130
20

70
50
60
4X Ø20
20
20
110
150
BOTTOM VIEW

P-101

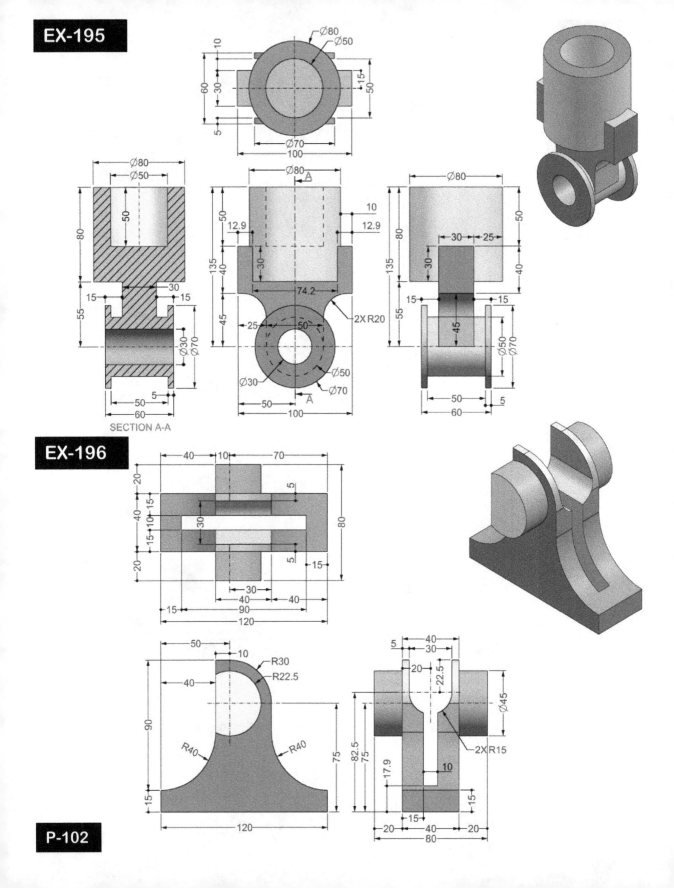

EX-195

⌀80
⌀50
10
60
30
15
50
5
⌀70
100

⌀80
⌀50
80
50
15
30
15
55
⌀30
⌀70
5
50
60
SECTION A-A

⌀80
A
50
10
12.9
12.9
135
30
40
74.2
45
25
50
2X R20
⌀30
⌀50
⌀70
50
A
100

⌀80
80
50
30
25
135
30
40
15
15
45
55
⌀50
⌀70
50
5
60

EX-196

40
10
70
20
40
15
10
5
80
30
15
20
5
15
30
40
40
15
90
120

50
10
R30
R22.5
40
90
R40
R40
75
15
120

5
40
30
20
22.5
⌀45
82.5
75
17.9
2X R15
10
15
15
20
40
20
80

P-102

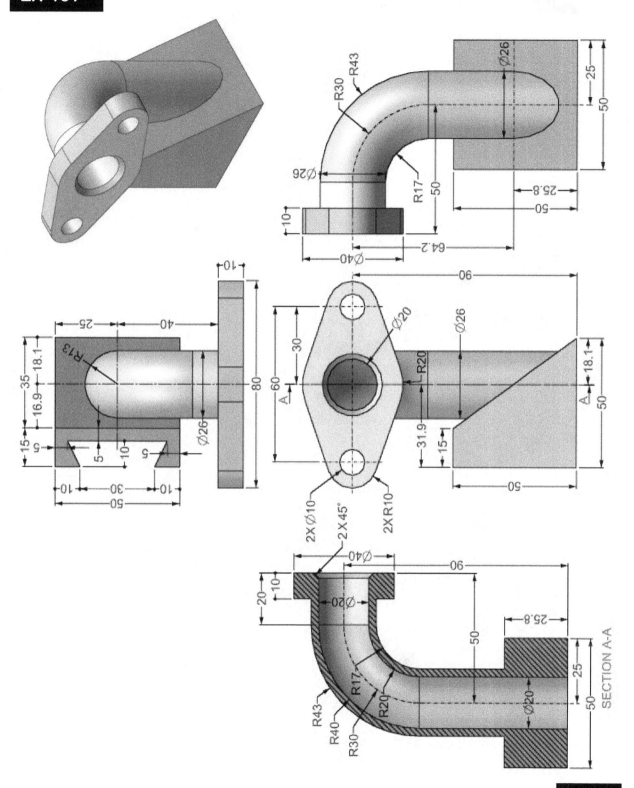

SECTION A-A

6X Ø15 THRU ON PCD 90

Ø120

Ø50

Ø40

PCD Ø90

A

A

VIEW B-B

8X Ø10 THRU ON PCD 54

Ø30

Ø70

Ø20

PCD Ø54

Ø120

Ø50

Ø40

15

10

Ø15

120

30

60°

80

Ø10

5

10

Ø20

Ø30

PCD 54

B-B

SECTION A-A

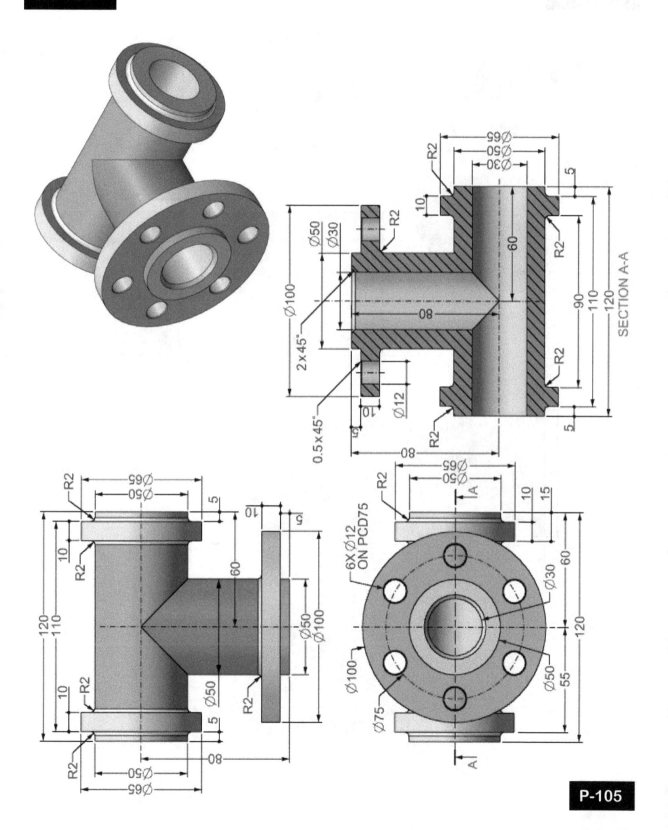

SECTION A-A

∅65
∅50
∅30
R2
5
10
60
R2
90
110
120
R2
R2
5
08
∅50
∅30
R2
∅100
2 x 45°
0.5 x 45°
10
5
∅12
R2

∅65
∅50
R2
5
10
R2
60
5
120
110
∅50
∅100
10
R2
R2
5
∅50
08
R2
∅65

∅65
∅50
R2
A
10
15
6X ∅12
ON PCD75
∅30
60
120
55
∅50
∅100
∅75
A

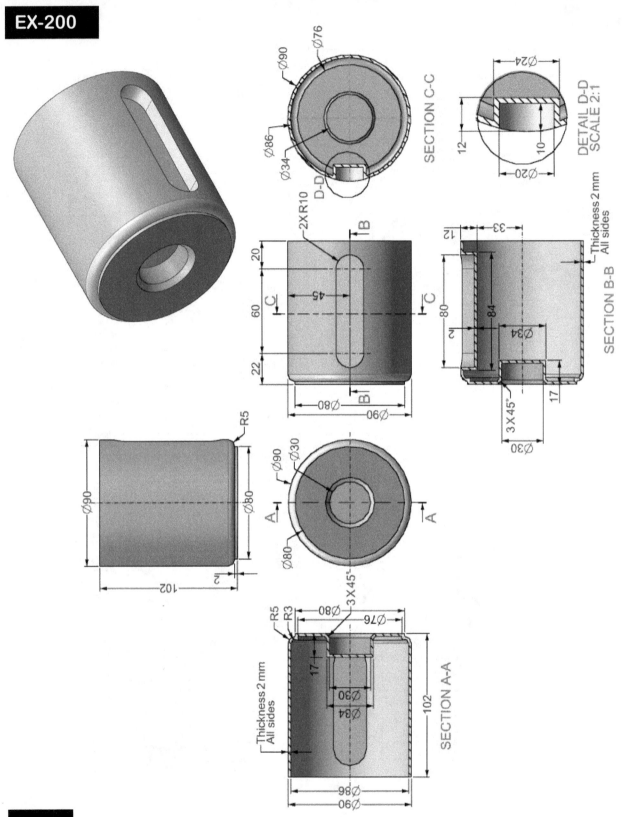

Ø76
Ø90
Ø86
Ø34
D-D
SECTION C-C

Ø24
12
10
Ø20
DETAIL D-D
SCALE 2:1
Thickness 2 mm
All sides

2XR10
B
20
C
45
60
C
22
B
Ø80
Ø90

33
12
80
84
2
Ø34
3X45°
17
Ø30
SECTION B-B
Thickness 2 mm
All sides

R5
Ø90
Ø80
102
2

Ø90
Ø30
A
A
Ø80

R5
R3
3X45°
Ø80
Ø76
17
Ø30
Ø84
102
Thickness 2 mm
All sides
Ø98
Ø90
SECTION A-A

Other useful books by CADIN360

1. 150 CAD Exercises

2. AutoCAD Exercises

3. CAD Exercises

4. 50+ SolidWorks Exercises

5. SolidWorks 200 Exercises

6. Autodesk Inventor Exercises

7. Catia Exercises

8. Siemens NX Exercises